I0033703

# Housing Codes for Repair and Maintenance

Using the General Police Power
and Minimum Housing Statutes to
Prevent Dwelling Deterioration

**C. Tyler Mulligan**

**Jennifer L. Ma**

UNC
SCHOOL OF
GOVERNMENT

The School of Government at the University of North Carolina at Chapel Hill works to improve the lives of North Carolinians by engaging in practical scholarship that helps public officials and citizens understand and improve state and local government. Established in 1931 as the Institute of Government, the School provides educational, advisory, and research services for state and local governments. The School of Government is also home to a nationally ranked graduate program in public administration and specialized centers focused on information technology, environmental finance, and civic education for youth.

As the largest university-based local government training, advisory, and research organization in the United States, the School of Government offers up to 200 courses, seminars, and specialized conferences for more than 12,000 public officials each year. In addition, faculty members annually publish approximately fifty books, book chapters, bulletins, and other reference works related to state and local government. Each day that the General Assembly is in session, the School produces the *Daily Bulletin*, which reports on the day's activities for members of the legislature and others who need to follow the course of legislation.

The Master of Public Administration Program is a full-time, two-year program that serves up to sixty students annually. It consistently ranks among the best public administration graduate programs in the country, particularly in city management. With courses ranging from public policy analysis to ethics and management, the program educates leaders for local, state, and federal governments and nonprofit organizations.

Operating support for the School of Government's programs and activities comes from many sources, including state appropriations, local government membership dues, private contributions, publication sales, course fees, and service contracts. Visit www.sog.unc.edu or call 919.966.5381 for more information on the School's courses, publications, programs, and services.

Michael R. Smith, Dean
Thomas H. Thornburg, Senior Associate Dean
Frayda S. Bluestein, Associate Dean for Faculty Development
Todd A. Nicolet, Associate Dean for Operations
Ann Cary Simpson, Associate Dean for Development
Bradley G. Volk, Associate Dean for Administration

Faculty

| | | |
|---|---|---|
| Gregory S. Allison | Willow S. Jacobson | William C. Rivenbark |
| David N. Ammons | Robert P. Joyce | Dale J. Roenigk |
| Ann M. Anderson | Kenneth L. Joyner | John Rubin |
| A. Fleming Bell, II | Diane M. Juffras | Jessica Smith |
| Maureen M. Berner | Dona G. Lewandowski | Karl W. Smith |
| Mark F. Botts | James M. Markham | Carl W. Stenberg III |
| Michael Crowell | Janet Mason | John B. Stephens |
| Shea Riggsbee Denning | Christopher B. McLaughlin | Charles Szypszak |
| James C. Drennan | Laurie L. Mesibov | Shannon H. Tufts |
| Richard D. Ducker | Kara A. Millonzi | Vaughn Upshaw |
| Joseph S. Ferrell | Jill D. Moore | Aimee N. Wall |
| Alyson A. Grine | Jonathan Q. Morgan | Jeffrey B. Welty |
| Norma Houston | Ricardo S. Morse | Richard B. Whisnant |
| Cheryl Daniels Howell | C. Tyler Mulligan | Gordon P. Whitaker |
| Jeffrey A. Hughes | David W. Owens | Eileen R. Youens |

© 2011 School of Government, The University of North Carolina at Chapel Hill

Use of this publication for commercial purposes or without acknowledgment of its source is prohibited. Reproducing, distributing, or otherwise making available to a non-purchaser the entire publication, or a substantial portion of it, without express permission, is prohibited.

Printed in the United States of America

25 24 23 22 21    3 4 5 6 7

ISBN 978-1-56011-662-2

Cover photo by Travis Long, The News & Observer

# Contents

# Introduction

Local government officials are all too familiar with the negative effects of a slowly deteriorating house. Neighbors complain as the front lawn gradually becomes overgrown, the exterior falls into unsightly (but not uninhabitable) disrepair, and the owner seems disinclined to do anything about it. Some residential structures deteriorate because they are vacant or abandoned, while others are occupied but neglected by the owners. The neighbors worry about the effect of such an eyesore on property values in the vicinity, about how far into decline the dwelling might slide, and about its ripple effects on the character of the community. The degree of disrepair may vary widely from complaint to complaint: from a house with merely an overgrown lawn and a broken ornamental light to a house with broken windows and a propensity to attract vagrants. In some cases, homeowners associations may be able to rely on restrictive covenants to police the condition of neighborhood homes, but even if these covenants are in place, enforcement may be too difficult or expensive for associations to undertake. It is not uncommon, therefore, for citizens to request local government assistance in addressing a problem with a deteriorating dwelling.[1]

Local governments, for their part, seek to regulate these dwellings for their own reasons: abating hazards to occupants and neighbors, maintaining property values (and therefore property tax revenue), eliminating blighting influences in a neighborhood, reducing crime, and preserving affordable housing stock, among others.[2] Local governing boards must therefore understand the limits of their regulatory authority.

To that end, this publication discusses the authority available under North Carolina law for local governments to address the problem of deteriorating dwellings, with a particular emphasis on repair-oriented intervention—in other words, intervention prior to the point at which a structure becomes so dilapidated that it is a better candidate for demolition than for repair.[3] Repair-oriented code enforcement occurs at an early stage in a dwelling's slide into disrepair; it is undertaken by local governments that are not content to stand idly by as dwellings deteriorate. These governments would prefer to maintain their housing stock in a reasonably good state of repair rather than wait until condemnation is necessary.

Once a dwelling is essentially beyond repair, of course, code enforcement must necessarily become more demolition-oriented, relying upon condemnation authority to eliminate the blighted structure. This publication will not address demolition-oriented code enforcement in much detail. The methods discussed herein, while applicable to all local governments, will be of greatest interest to local governments seeking to enact repair-oriented policies.

Another code enforcement topic that will not receive much treatment in this publication is building codes. While building codes will almost certainly be incorporated into any code enforcement program enacted by a local government, their primary purpose is to establish construction standards and, as a result, they tend to be less helpful with dwellings that were adequately constructed but have since been neglected. A deteriorating dwelling may exhibit outward appearance or other problems that are symptomatic of neglect before a building code violation can be observed or detected. The point of a repair-oriented code enforcement policy is to bring neglected and deteriorating dwellings to the attention of public officials sooner so that the dwellings can be repaired *before* they cause harm to occupants or the neighborhood. Such a policy requires going beyond building codes.

In North Carolina, other than the authority to preserve historic structures, there are two primary sources of statutory authority for repair-oriented residential code enforcement:[4] (1) the general police power for the regulation and abatement of "acts, omissions, or conditions, detrimental to the health, safety, or welfare of its citizens and the peace and dignity of the [city or county]"[5] and (2) minimum housing standards.[6] After dissecting and explaining the complex patchwork of statutes and case law from which these authorities are derived, this publication will explore how counties and cities can tailor local ordinances to meet specific needs.

Chapter 1 introduces the broad array of statutorily granted tools local governments might employ to deal with dwellings in varying stages of neglect. Chapter 2 elaborates on the general police power, the principal source of authority for regulating a dwelling when it first begins to deteriorate, and discusses how that power is limited by state statutes governing minimum housing standards (hereinafter "minimum housing statutes"). Chapter 3 then turns to the minimum housing statutes to examine their operation and limitations. Chapter 4 concludes by analyzing how the police power and minimum housing statutes can be applied together in the context of a hypothetical repair-oriented housing code.

## Notes

1. A dwelling, as the term is used in this publication, is owner-occupied or rental residential property. Dwellings can be single-family homes, multifamily residential buildings, and residential components of mixed-use structures. Buildings under construction are beyond the scope of this publication.

2. For an analysis of these local government rationales in the context of vacant dwellings, see C. Tyler Mulligan, *Toward a Comprehensive Program for Regulating Vacant or Abandoned Dwellings in North Carolina: The General Police Power, Minimum Housing Standards, and Vacant Property Registration*, 32 CAMPBELL L. REV. 1, 2–3 (2009), *available at* http://law.campbell.edu/lawreview/articles/32-1-1.pdf.

3. This publication expands on a similar analysis applied in the context of vacant property registration in Mulligan, note 2 above.

4. Code enforcement authority is also available for nonresidential buildings (see, e.g., N.C. GEN. STAT. (hereinafter G.S.) § 160A-439) and for historic structures (G.S. 160A-400.11 and G.S. 160A-400.14). This publication focuses on local government authority to regulate dwellings not designated as historic.

5. G.S. 160A-174(a) (cities) and G.S. 153A-121(a) (counties).

6. G.S. 160A-441 through G.S. 160A-450.

# 1
# Statutory Tools for Code Enforcement

Several different statutory tools are available to local governments that want to develop a code enforcement approach to the problem of deteriorating dwellings. These statutory options can be illustrated in the following example. Consider a house that suffers from owner neglect and gradually deteriorates over time. At each stage of deterioration, different types of local government authority for code enforcement come into play.

In the first stage, the imagined house is in good condition and not in any outward need of repair. A house in this stage will be called a "green condition" dwelling to indicate that it is in an acceptable state of repair. Although a local government may have legitimate reasons to monitor or regulate a green condition dwelling, particularly if it is vacant, no specific, comprehensive authority for such regulations is provided in the statutes.[1] If a North Carolina local government wishes to establish any sort of regulatory or monitoring program for green condition dwellings, it must devise its own regulations using its ordinance-making authority under the general police power.[2]

Suppose that the green condition dwelling described above is neglected by its owners and falls into a state of minor disrepair. Minor disrepair, for purposes of this publication, means the dwelling is structurally sound and still habitable; in other words, it is not yet *unfit for human habitation* (a defined term, associated with the minimum housing statutes, that will be explored in greater detail later).[3] This publication will refer to such a dwelling as a "yellow condition" dwelling to indicate that, although it exhibits visible signs of neglect or deterioration, it is still "fit for human habitation." The interests of a repair-oriented government with respect to a yellow condition dwelling include halting the decline of the dwelling, removing any visible signs of deterioration, inspecting the dwelling for potentially hazardous conditions, and restoring it to a green condition state of repair. As with green condition dwellings, no statute addresses these local government functions with respect to a yellow condition dwelling; a local government would need to develop its own regulatory program in reliance on the general police power.[4]

If the decline of a yellow condition dwelling is not halted, it may eventually become unfit for human habitation as defined in the minimum housing statutes.[5] A dwelling in this state is a "red condition" dwelling; it has deteriorated to the final stage at which code enforcement tools can likely preserve it. Unlike dwellings in green or yellow condition, dwellings in red condition can be addressed using a preexisting statutory scheme. In North Carolina, these unfit red condition dwellings are subject to local regulation pursuant to the minimum housing statutes.[6]

Dwellings that deteriorate further, to the point they become candidates for demolition, are in what this publication terms "black and blue condition." There is ample statutory authority for the initiation of condemnation proceedings for these dwellings, and in cases posing imminent danger, for summary demolition.

It is helpful to see these stages of deterioration in context with the full array of statutory grants of power. Table 1.1 summarizes the preceding discussion and provides an overview of the statutory tools available to local governments for code enforcement.

This publication focuses on repair-oriented code enforcement and therefore analyzes only regulatory activity directed at green, yellow, and red condition dwellings. It does not examine the regulation of black and blue dwellings. This limited scope is based on four premises. First, as a practical matter, dwellings in black and blue condition are unlikely to be renovated due to the high cost of repair. They may be, in fact, better candidates for demolition than for rehabilitation.[7] Second, as a corollary to the first point, code enforcement actions on green, yellow, and red condition dwellings are more likely to elicit the desired response from a dwelling owner (that is, repair and regular maintenance of the dwelling) because the cost of bringing such dwellings into full compliance with some standard of repair will be less for them than for black and blue dwellings. Third, code enforcement action against black and blue dwellings comes arguably too late to prevent the negative externalities—such as lower property values and damage to neighborhood character—that repair-oriented code enforcement is designed to prevent. Fourth, social theory explains that a house in decline will actually deteriorate more quickly once it is in a visible state of disrepair; thus, early intervention is necessary to preserve it. According to the "broken windows" sociological theory, highly contextual visible symbols

## Table 1.1. The Spectrum of Statutory Tools for Code Enforcement

| Dwelling Condition | Statute | Applicable When a Dwelling's Condition Is ... | Comments |
|---|---|---|---|
| Green | General police power to regulate conditions detrimental to the health, safety, or welfare of citizens and the peace and dignity of the [city or county] G.S. 160A-174(a) and G.S. 153A-121(a) | "detrimental to the health, safety, or welfare of [the] citizens and the peace and dignity of the city" | These dwellings are in good repair. Any monitoring of such green condition dwellings must be done under a local government's general police power. Chapter 2 discusses the general police power in detail. |
| Yellow | General police power (same as above) | "detrimental to the health, safety, or welfare of [the] citizens and the peace and dignity of the city" | These dwellings exhibit visible signs of disrepair that pose risks justifying regulation to halt the decline and restore the dwelling to green condition. |
| Red | Minimum housing standards G.S. 160A-441 through G.S. 160A-450 | "unfit for human habitation" | Local governments in North Carolina may utilize procedures established under the minimum housing statutes to regulate these dwellings. Chapter 3 discusses the minimum housing statutes in detail. |
| Black and blue (condemnation) | Condemnation G.S. 160A-426 through G.S. 160A-434 | "especially dangerous to life because of its liability to fire or because of bad conditions of the walls, overloaded floors, defective construction, decay, unsafe wiring or heating system, inadequate means of egress" | This statutory authority permits a local government to condemn property in this condition and order its repair, closing, or demolition as appropriate. |
| Black and blue (imminent danger) | Abatement of public health nuisances G.S. 160A-193 | "dangerous or prejudicial to the public health or public safety" | Cities are authorized to "summarily remove, abate, or remedy" public health nuisances and may summarily demolish dwellings if they pose an "imminent danger." Monroe v. City of New Bern, 158 N.C. App. 275, 278–79, 580 S.E.2d 372, 374–75 (2003). |

lead to epidemics of disorder if those symbols are not addressed early on.[8] In other words, if a few broken windows are not fixed, these visual symbols of blight signal to bad actors that no order is present, attracting (additional) vandalism and other criminal activity. Expanding this theory to a neighborhood context, a few houses in visible disrepair may lead to the decline of surrounding dwellings. The solution proposed by some is to fix the broken windows early on.[9] Indeed, North Carolina law explicitly permits governing boards to make findings consistent with the broken windows theory.[10] Based on these premises, local governments taking a repair approach will likely prefer early intervention and the immediate elimination of any visible signs of deterioration.

The remainder of this publication will explore how the available statutory power granted to North Carolina local governments[11] can be used to conduct code enforcement consistent with a repair-oriented approach.

## Notes

1. There is little statutory treatment of the regulation of green condition dwellings. When this publication went to print, the General Assembly had recently taken action to limit local government authority to register and inspect residential property in green condition. *See* Session Law 2011-281; *see also* Tyler Mulligan, "Residential Rental Inspection Programs: New Authority and Limitations," *Coates' Canons* (UNC School of Government blog), June 21, 2011, http://sogweb.sog.unc.edu/blogs/localgovt/?p=4842. The inspection limitations, however, do not restrict observations of the outside of residential buildings, so local governments are free to investigate and regulate the outward appearance of residential buildings as discussed in this publication. Additionally, the new law does not prohibit the registration and inspection of vacant buildings, particularly when all commercial and residential buildings are made subject to the same requirements. For an explanation of vacant property registration programs under North Carolina law, see C. Tyler Mulligan, *Toward a Comprehensive Program for Regulating Vacant or Abandoned Dwellings in North Carolina: The General Police Power, Minimum Housing Standards, and Vacant Property Registration*, 32 CAMPBELL L. REV. 1, 7 (2009), *available at* http://law.campbell.edu/lawreview/articles/32-1-1.pdf (discussing the rationales for a local government to enact a vacant property registration program and noting: "[A]ny vacant property, regardless of condition, presents a real risk to the community. There is therefore a legitimate government interest in maintaining awareness of a green condition dwelling's state of repair and in ensuring that the property remains well-maintained.").

2. All North Carolina local governments possess ordinance-making authority pursuant to their general police power. N.C. GEN. STAT. (hereinafter G.S.) § 160A-174(a) (cities) and G.S. 153A-121(a) (counties). For purposes of this publication, the general police power and the accompanying ordinance-making authority will be referred to collectively as the general police power.

3. See Section 3.1. Under North Carolina's minimum housing statutes, dwellings are defined as *unfit for human habitation* when they suffer from "defective conditions" such as "defects therein increasing the hazards of fire, accident, or other calamities; lack of adequate ventilation, light, or sanitary facilities; dilapidation; disrepair; structural defects; uncleanliness" which render the dwellings "dangerous or injurious to the health, safety or

morals of the occupants of the dwelling, the occupants of neighboring dwellings, or other residents of the city." G.S. 160A-444.

4. G.S. 160A-174(a) (cities) and G.S. 153A-121(a) (counties). An example of regulation of dwellings in green and yellow condition is a residential rental inspection program. *See* note 1, above.

5. See note 3 above.

6. G.S. 160A-441 through G.S. 160A-450.

7. Redevelopment strategies are more appropriate for black and blue properties, and those topics fall beyond the scope of this publication. Statutory authority for redevelopment exists under North Carolina's Urban Redevelopment Law, G.S. Ch. 160A, Article 22, and general redevelopment authority, G.S. 160A-457 (cities) and G.S. 153A-377 (counties).

8. *See* James Q. Wilson & George L. Kelling, *Broken Windows: The Police and Neighborhood Safety*, ATLANTIC MONTHLY, Mar. 1982; GEORGE L. KELLING & CATHERINE COLES, FIXING BROKEN WINDOWS: RESTORING ORDER AND REDUCING CRIME IN OUR COMMUNITIES (1996). With respect to vacant or abandoned properties, a sprinkling of neglected dwellings could lead to more widespread blight. *See* MALCOM GLADWELL, THE TIPPING POINT 141 (2000) ("If a window is broken and left unrepaired, people will conclude that no one cares and no one is in charge. Soon, more windows will be broken and the sense of anarchy will spread from the building to the street on which it faces, sending a signal that anything goes."). For a recent critique of the broken windows theory, see PETER K. B. ST. JEAN, POCKETS OF CRIME: BROKEN WINDOWS, COLLECTIVE EFFICACY, AND THE CRIMINAL POINT OF VIEW (2007). For a summary of some of the extensive recent research exploring the broken windows theory, see ST. JEAN, at 251–55 (Appendix B) (describing seven quantitative studies and three qualitative studies published between 1998 and 2003 about the broken windows theory and concluding that seven of the studies support the broken windows theory, two achieved mixed results, and one did not support the broken windows theory).

9. Early intervention is the solution suggested by the authors of the broken windows theory. *See* KELLING & COLES, note 8 above, at 251 ("From the earliest efforts to eliminate graffiti in the New York City subway, every department was involved and committed. Station managers monitored conditions in their stations continuously to ensure that minimum standards were maintained. Maintenance and repair staff cleaned new graffiti promptly, secured token receptacles, and repaired and cleaned facilities . . . The end result was not only order restored, but crime reduced, and most probably, prevented . . . Taking our cue from the New York experience, we believe that order-restoration and maintenance attempts are most effective and most likely to lead to crime prevention and reduction when a community mounts an integrated and comprehensive effort . . .").

10. *See* G.S. 160A-443(5a) and (5b) ("[I]f the governing body shall find . . . that the continuation of the dwelling in its vacated and closed status would . . . create a fire and safety hazard, would be a threat to children and vagrants, would attract persons intent on criminal activities, would cause or contribute to blight and the deterioration of property values in the area . . ."). *See also* G.S. 160A-425.1 and G.S. 160A-426 (authorizing an inspector to declare unsafe a vacant or abandoned nonresidential building if it "appears to the inspector to be in such dilapidated condition as to cause or contribute to blight, disease, vagrancy, fire or safety hazard, to be a danger to children, or to tend to attract persons intent on criminal activities or other activities that would constitute a public nuisance").

11. See Table 1.1.

# 2
# The General Police Power

Dwellings in green or yellow condition[1] are habitable, so a local government's primary concern with these dwellings is their outward appearance.[2] As discussed in the previous chapter, however, no statute grants specific authority to local governments to regulate the appearance of these dwellings. As a result, concerned local governments must rely upon their authority under the general police power and design their own regulations.[3] This chapter describes how local governments can employ the general police power for this purpose.

To begin, the chapter provides a brief introduction to the larger context in which North Carolina local governments function and are granted authority by the state. Against this backdrop, Section 2.2 explores how local governments can employ the general police power to enact repair-oriented code enforcement regulations. Because the efficacy of such regulations depends on a local government's ability to enforce them, Section 2.3 describes available enforcement mechanisms for regulations enacted pursuant to the general police power. Section 2.4 explains how costs associated with enforcement can be recouped. Finally, Section 2.5 discusses how local government authority is limited under state law, and more specifically, how the minimum housing statutes impose boundaries on the scope of the general police power in this instance.

## 2.1 Local Government Authority for the Exercise of the General Police Power

Local governments in North Carolina derive all their powers from delegation by the state.[4] The North Carolina constitution states: "The General Assembly . . . may give such powers and duties to counties, cities and towns, and other governmental subdivisions as it may deem advisable."[5] Thus, North Carolina local governments are creatures of legislative benevolence—not constitutional mandate.[6] It is therefore necessary to identify statutory authority for all activities undertaken by North Carolina local governments.

For actions taken pursuant to the general police power, North Carolina local governments rely upon a broad statutory grant of ordinance-making authority:

> [Cities and counties] may by ordinance define, prohibit, regulate, or abate acts, omissions, or conditions, detrimental to the health, safety, or welfare of its citizens and the peace and dignity of the [city or county], and may define and abate nuisances.[7]

This expansive language is fraught with ambiguity. How much authority did the legislature actually intend to grant to local governments? Interpreted broadly, this statute could be construed to authorize local governments to act on any issue tangentially related to local health, safety, welfare, peace, or dignity. Interpreted strictly or narrowly, however, the statute might be read to limit local government authority only to acts essential—not simply convenient, but indispensable—to local health, safety, welfare, or peace and dignity.

The courts have interpreted this language in various ways. Until the 1970s, North Carolina courts defined all grants of authority to local governments in very narrow terms under a strict construction scheme known as Dillon's rule.[8] However, in 1971 the North Carolina legislature enacted a call for broad interpretation of authorities granted to local governments:

> It is the policy of the General Assembly that the cities of this state should have adequate authority to execute the powers, duties, privileges, and immunities conferred upon them by law. To this end, the provisions of [Chapter 160A of the North Carolina General Statutes] and of city charters shall be broadly construed and grants of power shall be construed to include any additional and supplementary powers that are *reasonably necessary or expedient* to carry them into execution and effect: Provided, that the exercise of such additional or supplementary powers shall not be contrary to State or federal law or to the public policy of this State.[9]

A similar provision pertaining to counties was enacted in 1973.[10] North Carolina courts have not always heeded this explicit legislative call for broad construction, sometimes still applying a Dillon's rule form of strict construction.[11]

Given this ambiguity, will the police power be construed broadly or narrowly with respect to local government authority to enact repair-oriented code enforcement programs? Case law suggests that local governments would receive the benefit of broad construction. Even in the pre-1970s era of Dillon's rule strict interpretation by the courts, the general ordinance-making power of a city to "prevent nuisances"—even in the absence of specific state legislation—extended to regulation of the location of hog pens,[12] hospitals,[13] and gas storage.[14] Following the legislative call for broad interpretation of local government authority and despite the occasional application of Dillon's rule of strict construction by the courts, North Carolina case law evolved to grant increasingly extensive authority to local governments under the general police power.

The current test for examining the constitutional boundaries of police power regulation of private property was established by the North Carolina Supreme Court in *A-S-P Associates v. City of Raleigh*.[15] There the court employed an ends-means reasonableness test—in other words, it examined whether the means utilized by the local government were reasonably related to a legitimate government objective—to evaluate a comprehensive local ordinance governing aesthetic conditions in a historic district. In its analysis the court explained that a regulatory activity must first be within the scope of the general police power.[16] Once that is established, the regulation must meet a two-pronged test: "(1) Is the statute in its application reasonably necessary to promote the accomplishment of a public good and (2) is the interference with the owner's right to use his property as he deems appropriate reasonable in degree?"[17] The court answered these questions affirmatively for the ordinance at issue, but in doing so, it distinguished aesthetic regulation of historic property from other aesthetic regulation.[18] The court specifically declined to expand the scope of the police power to permit regulation for aesthetic purposes alone.[19]

The court's position changed in 1982 when, in *State v. Jones*, it determined that regulation of private property based on aesthetic considerations alone was a valid exercise of the police power.[20] This decision was consistent with the national trend during the second half of the twentieth century of judicial deference toward municipal police power.[21] In deciding *Jones*, which concerned a requirement for fencing around a junkyard, the court explored the permissibility of aesthetic regulations generally, stating:

> Aesthetic regulation may provide corollary benefits to the general community such as protection of property values, promotion of tourism, indirect protection of health and safety, preservation of the character and integrity of the community, and promotion of the comfort,

happiness, and emotional stability of area residents . . . . We therefore hold that reasonable regulation based on aesthetic considerations may constitute a valid basis for the exercise of the police power depending on the facts and circumstances of each case.[22]

The *Jones* court adopted essentially the same ends-means reasonableness test found in *A-S-P Associates*, but with some elaboration, describing a separate balancing test applicable when regulations are enacted solely for aesthetic purposes. The separate balancing test states that "the diminution in value of an individual's property should be balanced against the corresponding gain to the public from such regulation."[23] The court explained, "The test focuses on the reasonableness of the regulation by determining *whether the aesthetic purpose to which the regulation is reasonably related outweighs the burdens imposed on the private property owner by the regulation.*"[24] In weighing the burdens on the private property owner, factors to consider include whether the most substantial part of the value of the individual's property is confiscated or whether the individual is deprived of reasonable use of the property.[25] On the public benefit side of the equation, factors include the purpose of the regulation, the manner of achieving the permitted purpose,[26] and the corollary benefits to the general community quoted above, such as "protection of property values," "preservation of the character and integrity of the community," and "promotion of the comfort, happiness, and emotional stability of area residents."[27] For the junkyard fencing regulations in *Jones*, the court found that the balancing test weighed in the local government's favor.[28]

In evaluating local regulations governing the outward appearance of deteriorating dwellings, which test would a court apply? Would a court apply the stricter *State v. Jones* balancing test for aesthetic regulations, or would it apply the more generally applicable *A-S-P Associates* reasonableness test? An analysis of the purpose of repair-oriented regulations suggests that North Carolina courts would take the latter approach. As explained in Chapter 1, code enforcement activities designed to prevent deterioration of the outward appearance of dwellings are not undertaken in service of aesthetic purposes alone. Rather, improving the appearance of a deteriorating dwelling is intended to prevent many serious negative externalities, such as a depressing effect on neighboring property values and the possibility of increased crime, fire hazards, and blight.[29] When other than purely aesthetic purposes for regulations exist, courts have declined to apply the stricter *State v. Jones* balancing test and have instead used the *A-S-P Associates* reasonableness test.[30] One appellate panel relied simply on a local ordinance's findings and purpose clause to convince itself that an ordinance served more than purely aesthetic concerns.[31] Where non-aesthetic purposes are found, courts have turned to the *A-S-P Associates* test and had little difficulty finding an ordinance to be reasonably related to a legitimate public purpose.[32]

Although we cannot know for certain in the absence of case law directly on point, there is little reason to think the result would be different for regulations designed to prevent deterioration of dwellings. Nonetheless, an examination of repair-oriented regulations under the stricter *State v. Jones* balancing test will confirm the viability of such regulations. As demonstrated in the next section, repair-oriented regulations will likely hold up even under the more difficult test.

## 2.2 General Police Power Case Law as Applied to Repair-Oriented Regulations

In an effort to halt and reverse deterioration, repair-oriented regulations would likely address two different aspects of a deteriorating dwelling: (1) components contributing to structural soundness or safety and (2) nonstructural components and features that affect a dwelling's outward appearance.[33] Regulations in the first category—pertaining to structural soundness and safety—are generally the province of the minimum housing statutes, a point that will be discussed further in the final section of this chapter. Regulations in the second category—pertaining to the outward appearance of a dwelling—can be regulated only through the general police power and will be the focus of the balance of this chapter. Regulations in this second category are referred to as "good repair" regulations, since they require the outward appearance of a dwelling to be maintained in good repair.

As an example of a good-repair regulation intended to eliminate visible signs of deterioration, an owner might be required to repair an existing decorative fence with missing planks or to replace any damaged exterior ornamental light fixtures, even if such adorning items are not unsafe and serve only aesthetic purposes.[34] Since good-repair regulations address a dwelling's aesthetic, rather than structural, features, these regulations run the greatest risk of a court applying the stricter *Jones* analysis for aesthetic regulations rather than the *A-S-P Associates* ends-means reasonableness test. The analysis above suggests that the *A-S-P Associates* ends-means reasonableness test is the more appropriate test to apply to good-repair regulations, because such regulations serve more than just an aesthetic purpose.[35] But what if a court attempts to apply the stricter *State v. Jones* balancing test to a good-repair regulation or to some portion of it?

A good-repair regulation, such as a requirement that exterior ornamental light fixtures be kept in good repair for aesthetic reasons, would likely survive court scrutiny even if evaluated under the *State v. Jones* test. Weighing one side of the balancing test, a court would examine the gain to the public from the good-repair regulation. The court would likely find substantial public benefits of the type approved in *Jones*, such as "protection of property values"; "preservation of the character and integrity of the community"; "indirect protection of health and safety"; and the "promotion of the comfort, happiness, and emotional stability of area residents."

On the other side of the balance, a court would measure the "diminution in value of an individual's property" or the "burdens imposed on the private property owner" due to the good-repair regulation.[36] It would be difficult to argue that a good-repair regulation causes "diminution in value" of the regulated property. The value of a dwelling is normally sustained, if not increased, when it is well-maintained. And, in general, "the burdens imposed on the private property owner by the regulation" cannot be substantial. An owner—one who still occupies the dwelling or one who lives elsewhere—possesses some interest in maintaining the value of the property for rent or resale. A dwelling that remains functional and well-maintained holds greater value than a neglected property. One must therefore strain to argue that maintenance of a dwelling creates a private harm or an excessive burden for the owner.

That said, what if a private owner argues that she has idiosyncratic preferences against maintaining a dwelling in good repair and thus regulations requiring the maintenance of property in a certain manner inflict private burdens upon her which may outweigh the public gain? The courts are unlikely to sympathize with the owner. In deciding due process or takings challenges to municipal land use regulations, North Carolina courts are reluctant to find an ordinance unconstitutional even when the cost of compliance is prohibitive for the owner or when compliance causes hardship and inconvenience for a particular owner.[37]

A comparison to the facts in *State v. Jones* provides further support for this position. An owner might protest a requirement to expend funds for the repair and maintenance of a deteriorating dwelling, just as the junkyard owner in *State v. Jones* resisted the requirement to expend funds for the erection of a fence. The key finding in *State v. Jones*, however, was that the gain to the public from the aesthetic improvement alone outweighed this private burden borne by the junkyard owner.[38] Consider these facts in relationship to good-repair regulations in repair-oriented ordinances. The case for good-repair regulations is arguably more compelling than it is for the junkyard regulation in *Jones*. After all, the private owner of a dwelling reaps some personal benefit from maintaining its appearance, given that a dwelling's value is likely to be enhanced when its appearance is maintained rather than neglected. The junkyard owner, on the other hand, bore the expense of erecting a privacy fence for aesthetic purposes but likely gained little or no property value by doing so.[39] The benefit accrued almost entirely to the surrounding property owners and the public at large, yet the court upheld the aesthetic regulation.[40] Thus, good repair regulations applied to dwellings could possibly fare better under the *Jones* balancing test than regulations pertaining to the appearance of junkyards.

It is important to note that the *Jones* test permits a court to evaluate the facts and circumstances of a particular case.[41] One factual distinction that might be important to a court is whether a dwelling is owner-occupied. Consider, for example, a repair-oriented regulation directed at vacant or abandoned dwellings. It probably would not be difficult for a court to determine that the public gain from such a regulation outweighs the private burden on absentee owners who neglect their property.[42] A court might be more reluctant, however, to find that the public gain outweighs the private burden when a repair-oriented regulation is applied to an owner-occupied dwelling.[43] In that circumstance a court might accord more weight to the private burden prong of the *Jones* balancing test, or perhaps a court would be less likely to find such a regulation reasonable under the facts and circumstances of a particular case.[44] Because *State v. Jones* focused on junkyards—not dwellings, much less occupied dwellings—no judicial precedents clarify precisely how a North Carolina court would weigh the private burden in that context. However, in the absence of more specific North Carolina case law, it is reasonable to conclude that repair-oriented regulations would fall within the penumbra of a local government's police power authority, even when applied to owner-occupied dwellings.

Tenant-occupied dwellings deserve separate consideration. Residential rental property may be regulated pursuant to statutes authorizing local governments to regulate businesses and perform periodic inspections of problem properties, subject to some important limitations.[45] Several North Carolina local governments have employed the available authority to establish programs for inspecting residential rental property.[46]

Now, assuming that repair-oriented regulations were enacted by a local government pursuant to the general police power, would they be effective? The answer depends in part on available enforcement mechanisms and the local government's ability to fund administration and activities under the ordinance. These aspects of a repair-oriented code enforcement program are examined in the next two sections.

## 2.3 Enforcement of Local Government Ordinances Enacted under the General Police Power

Enforcement of ordinances is governed by Section 160A-175 of the North Carolina General Statutes (hereinafter G.S.) for municipalities and G.S. 153A-123 for counties. These statutes authorize three means of enforcement: (1) imprisonment; (2) fine or civil penalty; and (3) for conditions or uses on real property, by injunction or order of abatement. The maximum penalty may not exceed that set forth by G.S. 14-4.[47] At the time of this writing, the maximum penalty permitted is a $500 fine.[48] However, a local ordinance may provide that each day's continuing violation is a separate and distinct offense.[49] Therefore, these fines and penalties are potentially powerful enforcement tools, particularly given the means available to local governments to collect them.[50]

Of perhaps more interest in the case of repair-oriented regulations, however, is the power granted to local governments to compel property owners to comply with an ordinance, and, if a property owner refuses to comply, to effectuate compliance directly. This means that if an owner fails to make a repair required by a local ordinance, the local government can make the repair itself. To avail itself of this power, a local government must apply to the appropriate division of the General Court of Justice for an injunction and order of abatement.[51] An abatement order may cover a wide range of actions, including "that buildings or other structures on the property be closed, demolished, or removed; that fixtures, furniture, or other movable property be removed from buildings on the property; that grass and weeds be cut; that *improvements or repairs* be made; or that any other action be taken that is necessary to bring the property into compliance with the ordinance."[52]

If a violator refuses to comply with an abatement order, the local government may, through a contempt citation, obtain authority to effectuate the order itself.[53] The costs incurred by the government for effectuating the order become a lien on the violator's property, albeit a low-priority lien "in the nature of a mechanic's and materialman's lien."[54] Local government effectuation in this manner may achieve the desired result of a repaired dwelling, but it presents some practical difficulties. Legal proceedings are expensive, lengthy, and fraught with procedural complexity.[55] Additionally, collection of a low-priority lien is not always possible, so a local government must possess the financial means to pursue these remedies without being assured of collection.

## 2.4 Recoupment of Costs for Regulatory Activities under the General Police Power

Administration of repair-oriented regulations enacted under the general police power entails conducting inspections, effecting repairs, and complying with various procedural requirements. The costs associated with carrying out these activities are borne by the local government. The government's general fund may be tapped for this purpose, and revenue may be deposited back into the general fund from three potential sources. One was discussed in the preceding paragraph: the local government may recoup the costs of effectuating orders of abatement by collecting on associated liens.[56] The other two sources—fees for administration and civil penalties for owner noncompliance—will be discussed below. Fines are not included as a revenue source for reasons to be discussed later in this section.

### Fees

Fees may be imposed to defray the costs of administering a local government regulatory program.[57] In *Homebuilders Association of Charlotte, Inc. v. City of Charlotte*, the North Carolina Supreme Court upheld theimposition of user fees for a variety of city services, including special use permits, plat reviews, and building inspections, even though the city had no express statutory authority to levy the fees.[58] The city in that case held "express authority" to conduct the regulatory activities for which it was charging fees.[59] The court upheld the fees after applying the broad interpretation of local government authority called for by G.S. 160A-4, which includes "any additional and supplementary powers that are reasonably necessary or expedient" to perform the authorized activity.[60] However, the court also subjected such fees to a reasonableness test.[61] A rough estimate of reasonableness is the amount necessary to meet the full cost of the particular regulatory program.[62]

Would fees charged in the administration of good-repair regulations be upheld, assuming they are set at a reasonable level? Probably so. As discussed in Section 2.2, North Carolina case law leaves little doubt that local governments may enact good-repair regulations. The case law is arguably tantamount to express authority, and statutes already authorize fees for rental property registration programs under certain conditions, making it reasonable to conclude that administrative fees associated with good-repair regulations are authorized.[63]

### Civil Penalties

As discussed in Section 2.3, civil penalties may be assessed against an owner who violates a local government ordinance. Penalties can be as high as $500 per violation, with each day's continuing violation constituting a separate offense. However, if a local government seeks to retain the proceeds from civil penalties in order to partially offset the costs of administering its code enforcement program, the penalties must be designed with care and probably cannot be set at the maximum amount allowed by law.

Ordinarily, fines—and in some instances civil penalties—are required by the state constitution to be paid over to the school system when they are intended to be penal in nature—that is, when they are collected for "any breach of the penal laws."[64] Fines are usually associated with criminal citations and are therefore characterized as penal in nature—they must be paid over to the school system in every instance. Civil penalties, however, can avoid this characterization and may be retained by a local government if (1) the scope of the penalty is limited such that it accomplishes restitution only for actual damages and compliance costs and (2) enforcement through criminal citation is prohibited (in other words, the ordinance expressly states that enforcement consists solely of civil penalties and injunctive relief). This general framework is based on a nuanced interpretation of North Carolina case law.[65] Local governments are advised to consult their attorneys when crafting any civil penalty with the intent of retaining the proceeds.

## 2.5 Limitations on the General Police Power: Encroaching on the Minimum Housing Statutes

Thus far this chapter has described how North Carolina local governments may conduct repair-oriented regulatory activities pursuant to their general police power by enacting regulations requiring dwellings to be maintained in good repair, with a focus on outward appearance. In the case of green and yellow condition dwellings, this ends the analysis of local government authority, because the general police power is the primary authority available for imposing repair and maintenance standards on these dwellings.[66]

In the case of red condition dwellings—dwellings unfit for human habitation[67]—the analysis must continue. The General Assembly has granted to local governments separate statutory authority, through the minimum housing statutes, applicable only to this class of dwellings. Thus two sources of statutory authority are available for the regulation of red condition dwellings: the general police power, which is broad enough to authorize the regulation of dwellings in any condition, and the minimum housing statutes, which apply only to red condition dwellings. This section explores the interplay between the general police power and the minimum housing statutes and describes how the minimum housing statutes essentially limit the applicability of the general police power in the case of red condition dwellings.

When a North Carolina local government is authorized to perform an activity by more than one statute, generally the local government may use any or all of those statutes as the basis for its authority to act.[68] However, some specific grants of authority impose precise requirements on local governments that may trump a more general power as a matter of statutory interpretation, particularly where a regulation adopted under a general power is "repugnant" to a more specific grant of authority.[69] In the context of repair-oriented regulations, minimum housing statutes raise precisely this issue. These statutes offer a rather precise statutory scheme for the regulation of red condition dwellings, thereby raising the question of whether alternative procedures adopted under the general police power are authorized.

The North Carolina Court of Appeals appears to have answered the question in the negative, as it has looked unfavorably upon local regulatory activities found inconsistent with the precise requirements of the minimum housing statutes.[70] In *Newton v. City of Winston-Salem*, the North Carolina Court of Appeals held that a local government must follow the procedural requirements of the minimum housing statutes when regulating dwellings unfit for human habitation, declaring that "[t]he statute specifically states that cities and counties may exercise such powers *only* 'in the manner herein provided.'"[71] The court, in making this finding, noted the statutory requirement that "an ordinance adopted by a city to regulate buildings unfit for human habitation 'shall contain' certain provisions" included in the minimum housing statutes.[72]

The *Newton* decision accords with accepted principles of statutory construction. Specifically, the minimum housing statutes provide detailed procedural protections for owners of unfit dwellings,[73] protections that would be eviscerated if local governments could simply act under the general police power. To permit a local government to evade these procedural protections would either be repugnant to the minimum housing statutes[74] or would violate the canon requiring statutes to be interpreted in a way that avoids making a provision meaningless.[75] Therefore, to lend meaning to the state's minimum housing statutes, local governments must utilize the procedures set forth in those statutes when establishing regulations governing the repair of dwellings that are "unfit for human habitation" (in this publication, red condition dwellings).

How do the general police power and minimum housing statutes apply in the case of a red condition dwelling that simultaneously exhibits conditions rendering it "unfit for human habitation" (such as a gaping hole in the roof) and conditions that do *not* contribute to its "unfit" state (such as damaged ornamental exterior light fixtures)? Does the fact that the dwelling is classified in red condition and unfit for human habitation require that the procedures set forth in the minimum housing statutes be applied to all repairs, however minor or aesthetic? Or should the minimum housing statutes' procedures be applied only to repairs pertaining to a dwelling's fitness, or unfitness, for human habitation? Examination of the statute suggests it must be the latter. The plain language of the minimum housing statutes permits a local government to issue an order for the repair of a dwelling "*in order to render it fit* for human habitation."[76] Repairs that do not make the dwelling fit are outside the scope of this order.

Accordingly, minimum housing statutes are themselves limited in scope, extending only to conditions that, if repaired, would "render [a dwelling] fit for human habitation."[77] This leaves room for a separate set of regulations,[78] addressing the outward appearance of a dwelling, to sit alongside minimum housing regulations. Therefore a red condition dwelling could conceivably be regulated by two schemes at once. Aspects of the dwelling that render it unfit for human habitation would be regulated pursuant to the minimum housing statutes; the outward appearance would be covered by good-repair regulations enacted pursuant to the general police power.

Table 2.1 illustrates the division of authority between the general police power and the minimum housing statutes.

In summary, local governments seeking to regulate green or yellow condition dwellings would enact regulations based solely upon the general police power. With respect to red condition structures, the statutory

**Table 2.1. Applicability of the General Police Power and Minimum Housing Statutes**

| | Authority for regulating conditions not determinative of a dwelling's fitness or unfitness for human habitation (for example, good-repair regulations pertaining to outward appearance) | Authority for regulating substandard conditions determinative of a dwelling's fitness or unfitness for human habitation |
|---|---|---|
| Green condition dwellings | General police power | Not applicable |
| Yellow condition dwellings | General police power | Not applicable |
| Red condition dwellings | General police power | Minimum housing statutes |

authority applied would depend upon the condition: regulations governing conditions that pertain to a dwelling's fitness or unfitness for human habitation must adhere to the procedures set forth in the state's minimum housing statutes, whereas good-repair regulations (covering conditions with no bearing on the fitness of a dwelling) would be based upon the general police power.

It is impossible to delineate a precise boundary between the dwelling conditions that fall under the purview of the minimum housing statutes and those that are subject to the general police power, primarily because the coverage of the minimum housing statutes is flexible. By statute, local governments are permitted to adjust or manipulate the definition of *unfit for human habitation*. Conditions defined as unfit for human habitation in one community might not be defined as unfit in another. Thus each local government can expand or narrow the scope of conditions covered by its minimum housing ordinance, thereby making the outer boundary of the minimum housing statutes impossible to pin down.[79] Chapter 3 examines this facet of the minimum housing statutes further and discusses their general operation.

## Notes

1. Green condition and yellow condition dwellings are defined in Chapter 1.

2. References to "appearance," and later to "aesthetic," regulation are made in the sense of maintaining the existing aesthetic features of dwellings—for example, keeping the outward appearance of a dwelling in good order, regardless of design or architectural style. These are not references to zoning-based appearance and aesthetic regulations such as architectural style, required design features, and other nonmaintenance requirements such as buffer zones, landscaping, or open space. This point is further explained in the discussion of good-repair regulations in Section 2.2. It should be noted that the outward appearance of most dwellings can be observed from outside the property, so authority to conduct inspections is not a necessary component of regulatory programs governing green and yellow condition dwellings. However, limited authority to conduct inspections of green and

yellow condition dwellings is provided in N.C. Gen. Stat. (hereinafter G.S.) § 160A-424 (cities) and G.S. 153A-364 (counties).

3. G.S. 160A-174 (cities) and G.S. 153A-121 (counties).

4. For a discussion of municipal authority and its evolution in North Carolina, see Frayda S. Bluestein, *Do North Carolina Local Governments Need Home Rule?*, 84 N.C. L. Rev. 1983, 1989–90 (2006). *See also* David Owens, *Local Government Authority to Implement Smart Growth Programs: Dillon's Rule, Legislative Reform and the Current State of Affairs in North Carolina*, 35 Wake Forest L. Rev. 671, 680–82 (2000); A. Fleming Bell, II, *Dillon's Rule Is Dead; Long Live Dillon's Rule!*, Loc. Gov't L. Bull. No. 66 (Mar. 1995).

5. N.C. Const. art. VII, § 1.

6. A. Fleming Bell, II, *Article 4: The Police Power, in* County and Municipal Government in North Carolina at 2, *available at* www.sog.unc.edu/pubs/cmg/cmg04 .pdf ("North Carolina is not a 'home rule' state, as that term is commonly understood. Its local governments exist by legislative benevolence, not by constitutional mandate.").

7. G.S. 160A-174(a) (cities) and G.S. 153A-121(a) (counties).

8. *See* Bluestein, note 4 above, at 2011. Under Dillon's rule, a local government may exercise only three types of powers: (1) those granted to it by the legislature in express words; (2) those "necessarily or fairly implied in, or incident to the powers expressly granted"; and (3) those "essential to the declared objects and purposes of the corporation— not simply convenient, but indispensable." *Id.* (quoting John F. Dillon, Treatise on the Law of Municipal Corporations 101–02 (1872)).

9. G.S. 160A-4 (emphasis added).

10. G.S. 153A-4.

11. *See* Bluestein, note 4 above, at 2012 ("North Carolina courts have not consistently heeded this legislative directive to construe broadly local-enabling legislation. Instead, courts have intermittently applied Dillon's rule and other limiting rules of construction.").

12. State v. Hord, 122 N.C. 1092, 29 S.E. 952 (1898).

13. Lawrence v. Nissen, 173 N.C. 359, 91 S.E. 1036 (1917).

14. Gulf Ref. Co. v. McKernan, 179 N.C. 314, 102 S.E. 505 (1920) (upholding a Sanford ordinance prohibiting aboveground storage of kerosene or gasoline within 1,000 feet of any dwelling).

15. 298 N.C. 207, 214, 258 S.E.2d 444, 448–49 (1979) ("Several principles must be borne in mind when considering a due process challenge to governmental regulation of private property on grounds that it is an invalid exercise of the police power. First, is the object of the legislation within the scope of the police power? Second, considering all the surrounding circumstances and particular facts of the case is the means by which the governmental entity has chosen to regulate reasonable?" (citations omitted)).

16. *Id.*

17. *Id.*

18. *Id.* at 216, S.E.2d at 450.

19. *Id.* (taking note of "the growing body of authority in other jurisdictions recognizing that the police power may be broad enough to include reasonable regulation of property for aesthetic reasons alone" but not endorsing "such a broad concept of the scope of the police power").

20. 305 N.C. 520, 530–31, 290 S.E.2d 675, 681–82 (1982) (finding that a local government's ordinance requiring fencing around a junkyard for aesthetic reasons was a valid exercise of the police power).

21. See John P. Dwyer & Peter S. Menell, Property Law and Policy: A Comparative Institutional Perspective 919 (1998) ("After the *Euclid* Court (Village of Euclid v. Ambler Realty Co., 272 U.S. 365, (1926)) held that municipalities could, consistent with due process, invoke the police power to regulate private land use, the balance of power between

the community's right to shape land use and individual property and civil rights shifted dramatically in favor of municipal authority. Highly deferential judicial review as well as the underlying logic of *Euclid* quickly led municipalities not only to regulate uses that directly affected health and welfare, but also to regulate or even prohibit uses that reflect individual aesthetic judgment . . ."). Prior to *Euclid*, most state courts held that the police power did not extend to aesthetic regulation. *Id.*

22. State v. Jones, 305 N.C. 520, 530–31, 290 S.E.2d 675, 681 (1982).

23. *Jones*, 305 N.C. at 530, 290 S.E.2d at 681. This language first appears without elaboration in *A-S-P Associates,* almost as an aside. A-S-P Assocs. v. City of Raleigh, 298 N.C. 207, 218, 258 S.E.2d 444, 451 (1979).

24. *Jones*, 305 N.C. at 530, 290 S.E.2d at 681. Although the test articulated in *Jones* can be viewed as merely an elaboration of the *A-S-P Associates* test, the italicized language and the accompanying factors are frequently treated as an independent test for aesthetic regulations. *See, e.g.,* Summey Outdoor Adver., Inc. v. Cnty. of Henderson, 96 N.C. App. 533, 540–41, 386 S.E.2d 439, 444 (1989); Capital Outdoor, Inc. v. Tolson, 159 N.C. App. 55, 62, 582 S.E.2d 717, 722 (2003); Quality Built Homes, Inc. v. Village of Pinehurst, 2008 WL 3503149 (M.D.N.C.), at 8. The *Jones* balancing test will therefore be distinguished from the *A-S-P Associates* reasonableness test for purposes of this publication.

25. *Jones*, 305 N.C. at 530, 290 S.E.2d at 681.

26. *Id.*

27. *Id.*

28. State v. Jones, 305 N.C. 520, 530–31, 290 S.E.2d 675, 681–82 (1982) (holding that the "ordinance in instant case" is a valid exercise of the police power).

29. See Introduction and Chapter 1 (addressing early intervention by local governments for a dwelling falling into disrepair). Most of the discussion surrounding negative externalities resulting from deteriorating dwellings has centered on foreclosed or vacant properties. These dwellings depress the values of neighboring properties, foster criminal activity, and push neighborhoods into decline. *See, e.g.,* CENTER FOR RESPONSIBLE LENDING, SOARING SPILLOVER: ACCELERATING FORECLOSURES TO COST NEIGHBORS $502 BILLION IN 2009 ALONE (May 2009), www.responsiblelending.org/mortgage-lending/ research-analysis/soaring-spillover-3-09.pdf; KAI-YAN LEE, FORECLOSURE'S PRICE-DEPRESSING SPILLOVER EFFECTS ON LOCAL PROPERTIES: A LITERATURE REVIEW, Fed. Res. Bank of Boston, Community Affairs Discussion Paper No. 2008-01 (2008), *available at* www.bos.frb.org/commdev/pcadp/2008/pcadp0801.pdf (providing an overview of the price effects of foreclosure); DAN IMMERGLUCK & GEOFF SMITH, THE IMPACT OF SINGLE-FAMILY MORTGAGE FORECLOSURES ON NEIGHBORHOOD CRIME 16 (2005), *available at* www.woodstockinst.org/publications/download/the-impact-of-single-family-mortgage-foreclosures-on-neighborhood-crime/ (finding that each foreclosure in a 100-house neighborhood corresponded to a 2.33 percent increase in violent crime, holding all other factors constant). Vacant dwellings have also been connected to increased risk of fire and fire injuries. Donna Shai, *Income, Housing, and Fire Injuries: A Census Tract Analysis,* 121 PUBLIC HEALTH REP. 149, 151 (Mar.–Apr. 2006), *available at* www.pubmedcentral.nih. gov/articlerender.fcgi?artid=1525262#id523188. Local governments have had to expend additional government resources in the form of more frequent police patrols and code inspections to combat the effects of slowly deteriorating vacant housing. *See* Patrick Jonsson, *Vacant Homes Spread Blight in Suburb and City Alike,* CHRISTIAN SCIENCE MONITOR, July 1, 2008, § USA, at 1 ("Boarded-up homes are an expensive problem for Atlanta, which has already posted 'no trespass' signs at as many homes this year as in all of last year. . . With 11 code enforcers laid off because of budget cuts, Atlanta police are working overtime to patrol blighted streets. 'The responsibility is falling more heavily on our shoulders,' says Atlanta Police Maj. Joseph Dallas.").

30. *See, e.g.,* Summey Outdoor Adver., Inc. v. Cnty. of Henderson, 96 N.C. App. 533, 540–41, 386 S.E.2d 439, 444 (1989) ("We find Jones to be inapplicable to the case at bar, because the ordinance in question is not for aesthetics only."). *See also* Capital Outdoor, Inc. v. Tolson, 159 N.C. App. 55, 62, 582 S.E.2d 717, 722 (2003) (declining to apply *State v. Jones* balancing test to billboard height regulations because they addressed safety concerns as well as an aesthetic purpose).

31. *Summey,* 96 N.C. App. at 540, 386 S.E.2d at 444 ("Furthermore, we rely on Article II of the ordinance where aesthetics is listed as only one of several purposes.").

32. *See, e.g., Summey,* 96 N.C. App. at 541–42, 386 S.E.2d at 444; *Capital Outdoor,* 159 N.C. App. at 62, 582 S.E.2d at 722.

33. A further distinction is implied between two different types of regulations governing the outward appearance of a dwelling: (1) those requiring the outward appearance of *existing* dwelling components and features to be maintained, such as requiring an existing fence, existing light fixture, or existing accessory building to be maintained in good repair and (2) those imposing architectural or landscaping appearance regulations on *new* construction, such as paint color, number of trees, or aesthetic design requirements. This publication focuses on existing dwellings and thus is concerned only with the former. For an exploration of architectural and landscaping regulations, which is beyond the scope of this publication, see *Quality Built Homes, Inc. v. Village of Pinehurst,* 2008 WL 3503149 (M.D.N.C.) (undertaking a *Jones* analysis and upholding an ordinance including architectural and landscaping requirements following a determination that the municipality presented sufficient evidence of corollary benefits and that the cost of compliance was not "so prohibitive that the burden to [the property owners] outweighs the benefits to the community").

34. Other examples of aesthetic conditions that might be targeted by repair-oriented code enforcement include removal of graffiti, maintenance of accessory buildings in a state of good repair, maintenance of driveways and sidewalks in good repair, repair of peeling or chipping paint, removal of noncombustible rubbish from the premises, yard maintenance to a neighborhood standard, and repair of cracked (but intact) window panes.

35. See notes 29–32 above and accompanying text.

36. State v. Jones, 305 N.C. 520, 530, 290 S.E.2d 675, 681 (1982).

37. *See* Responsible Citizens in Opposition to Flood Plain Ordinance v. City of Asheville, 308 N.C. 255, 265, 302 S.E.2d 204, 210 (1983) ("Even assuming that the cost of complying with the land-use regulations is prohibitive (and we do not decide that it is) and recognizing that the market value of plaintiffs' properties has diminished (a fact found by the trial court), these factors are of no consequence here. As this Court noted in *A-S-P Associates v. City of Raleigh,* 'the mere fact that an ordinance results in the depreciation of the value of an individual's property or restricts to a certain degree the right to develop it as he deems appropriate is not sufficient reason to render the ordinance invalid.'") (citations omitted); *In re* Parker, 214 N.C. 51, 55, 197 S.E. 706, 710 (1938) ("The petitioner complains that the ordinance is an arbitrary and unreasonable restriction upon the petitioner's property rights. That he, due to the particular circumstances of his case, may suffer hardship and inconvenience by an enforcement of the ordinance is not sufficient ground for invalidating it. The fact that the ordinance is harsh and seriously depreciates the value of complainant's property is not enough to establish its invalidity.") (citations omitted). *See also* Summey Outdoor Adver., Inc. v. Cnty. of Henderson, 96 N.C. App. 533, 542, 386 S.E.2d 439, 445 (1989) ("The fact that it will be costly for plaintiff to bring some of his signs into compliance with the ordinance does not rise to the level of an interference with his right to *use* the property as he deems fit."). These North Carolina cases are consistent with U.S. Supreme Court decisions. *See* Penn Cent. Transp. Co. v. New York City, 438 U.S. 104, 138 (1978) (holding that New York City's restrictions on the development of historic landmarks such

as Grand Central Terminal were constitutionally permissible and were not a "taking" because "[t]he restrictions imposed are substantially related to the promotion of the general welfare" and still permitted reasonable beneficial use of the property). In its analysis, the Court defers to legislative determinations of public interest, overriding individual real property interests: "[I]n instances in which a state tribunal reasonably concluded that 'the health, safety, morals, or general welfare' would be promoted by prohibiting particular contemplated uses of land, this Court has upheld land-use regulations that destroyed or adversely affected recognized real property interests." *Id.* at 125. The Court specifically notes: "States and cities may enact land-use restrictions or controls to enhance the quality of life by preserving the character and desirable aesthetic features of a city." *Id.* at 129 (citations omitted).

38. *Jones*, 305 N.C. at 530–31, 290 S.E.2d at 681–82.

39. Valuation of commercial property—such as a junkyard—is based primarily upon income or comparables and is unlikely to be changed significantly by the presence of a privacy fence. One can imagine possible exceptions to the rule—a particularly effective or attractive privacy fence might make a junkyard more viable over the long run because it will be less likely to attract the attention or ire of neighbors—but the privacy fence may not necessarily translate into additional value in the same way a dwelling's value is enhanced when its appearance is maintained. In other words, "curb appeal" is probably more important to the value of a private dwelling than it is to the value of a junkyard.

40. *Jones*, 305 N.C. at 530–31, 290 S.E.2d at 681–82.

41. *Jones*, 305 N.C. at 530–31, 290 S.E.2d at 681 (1982) ("We therefore hold that *reasonable* regulation based on aesthetic considerations *may* constitute a valid basis for the exercise of the police power *depending on the facts and circumstances of each case*.") (emphasis added).

42. For an analysis of these tests as applied to vacant or abandoned dwellings, see C. Tyler Mulligan, *Toward a Comprehensive Program for Regulating Vacant or Abandoned Dwellings in North Carolina: The General Police Power, Minimum Housing Standards, and Vacant Property Registration*, 32 Campbell L. Rev. 1 (2009), *available at* http://law.campbell.edu/lawreview/articles/32-1-1.pdf.

43. For recent perspectives on the home's special status in the law, see Stephanie M. Stern, *Residential Protectionism and the Legal Mythology of Home*, 107 Mich L. Rev. 1093 (2009); Jeannie Suk, *Taking the Home*, 20 Cardozo Stud. L. & Lit. 291 (2008).

44. In the more likely scenario that the regulation is evaluated under the *A-S-P Associates* test, compare notes 15–19 above and accompanying text.

45. Local government inspection departments are authorized to conduct periodic building inspections for unlawful or unsafe conditions as provided in G.S. 160A-424 (cities) and G.S. 153A-364 (counties). Local governments may regulate and license businesses pursuant to G.S. 160A-194 (cities) and G.S. 153A-134 (counties). Landlords must provide fit premises pursuant to G.S. 42-42. Any program for the inspection of residential building interiors by city or county inspections departments must conform with the limitations set forth in G.S. 160A-424 and G.S. 153A-364. See Chapter 1, note 1. Separate inspection authority under the minimum housing statutes is discussed in Chapter 3, note 12.

46. For a discussion of rental inspection programs in North Carolina, see Carol Cooley Hickey, Ensuring Housing Quality: Proactive Minimum Housing Code Inspections of Rental Properties in North Carolina Cities (2008) (M.P.A. student capstone paper, UNC Chapel Hill School of Government), *available at* www.sog.unc.edu/uncmpa/students/documents/CarolHickey.pdf. *See also* Godwin v. City of Dunn, No. 5:09-CV-381-80, 2010 WL 2813513 (E.D.N.C. July 16, 2010) (upholding a rental inspection program without addressing the question of local government authority). The aforementioned programs were first enacted prior to S.L. 2011-281, which places limits on local government authority to conduct periodic inspections of the interior of residential properties without reasonable

cause to believe a code violation or hazardous condition exists in the residence. However, S.L. 2011-281 does not prohibit all registration and inspection programs. Programs that monitor the *outward* appearance of structures or that govern vacant properties are largely unrestricted. See Chapter 1, note 1.

47. *See* G.S. 160A-175(b) (municipalities) and G.S. 153A-123(b) (counties).

48. *See* G.S. 14-4.

49. *See* G.S. 160A-175(g), G.S. 153A-123(g).

50. *See, e.g.,* G.S. Chapter 105A (Setoff Debt Collection Act).

51. G.S. 160A-175(e), G.S. 153A-123(e).

52. *Id.* (emphasis added).

53. *Id.*

54. *Id.*

55. Compliance by the local government with the enforcement process is a difficult task in itself. Describing a process not atypical across the nation, one author explains it this way: "If a code enforcement attorney wants to obtain a judicial order mandating the owner to correct the violations, the attorney must first show the court that the owner has been personally served with notice of the case. A subsequent finding of contempt for failure to obey the order would require proof that the owner actually knew that the order had been made. A speculating owner can frustrate attempts at personal service by creating sham ownership entities or just by providing a vacant house as the only mailing address for himself as owner of the property. Although the owner may be unable to achieve complete anonymity, he may succeed in making pursuit of him just difficult enough to induce a code enforcement attorney to use the agency's limited resources on a more attainable defendant." James J. Kelly, Jr., *Refreshing the Heart of the City: Vacant Building Receivership as a Tool for Neighborhood Revitalization and Community Empowerment*, 13 J. Affordable Hous. & Cmty. Dev. L. 210, 214 (2004).

56. See note 54 above and accompanying text.

57. *See* Homebuilders Ass'n of Charlotte, Inc. v. City of Charlotte, 336 N.C. 37, 46, 442 S.E.2d 45, 51 (1994) (concluding that a city has authority to assess user fees for a variety of governmental regulatory services provided such fees are reasonable).

58. *Homebuilders*, 336 N.C. at 42, 442 S.E.2d at 49 ("The generally accepted rule today seems to be that the municipal power to regulate an activity implies the power to impose a fee in an amount sufficient to cover the cost of regulation."). *See also* David W. Owens, Land Use Law in North Carolina 18–19 (2006).

59. *Homebuilders*, 336 N.C. at 43, 442 S.E.2d at 49 ("Thus, in this case, the services for which user fees are charged are all related to some express authority of the City to regulate the development of land.").

60. *Homebuilders*, 336 N.C. at 43, 442 S.E.2d at 50.

61. *Homebuilders*, 336 N.C. at 46, 442 S.E.2d at 51 ("Even though we conclude that the City does have the authority to assess user fees to defray the costs of regulation, such fees will not be upheld if they are unreasonable.").

62. *Id.*

63. Any fees levied against residential properties must comply with statutory requirements. *See* S.L. 2011-281 (modifying G.S. 160A-424 (cities) and 153A-364 (counties) and prohibiting levying any fees against residential rental properties that are not also levied against other residential and commercial properties, with an exception for rental properties that are identified as problem properties). See also Chapter 1, note 1.

64. N.C. Const. art. IX, § 7.

65. *See, e.g.,* N.C. Sch. Bds. Ass'n v. Moore, 359 N.C. 474, 614 S.E.2d 504 (2005). *See also* David M. Lawrence, *Fines, Penalties, and Forfeitures: An Historical and Comparative Analysis*, 65 N.C. L. Rev. 49 (1986); Shea Riggsbee Denning, *Public School Funding in the*

*Summer of 2005:* North Carolina Sch. Bds. Ass'n v. Moore, LOCAL GOV'T L. BULL. NO. 108 (School of Government, Nov. 2005); DAVID W. OWENS, LAND USE LAW IN NORTH CAROLINA 179 (2006).

66. See Chapter 1, notes 2–4 and accompanying text.

67. See Chapter 1, note 6 and accompanying text.

68. G.S. 153A-3 and G.S. 160A-3. *See also* Bell, note 6 above, at 5 ("In many of those cases in which a city or county is authorized to carry out a particular activity by more than one statute, the local government may use any of them as its authorization").

69. *See* Krauss v. Wayne Cnty. Dep't of Soc. Servs., 347 N.C. 371, 378–79, 493 S.E.2d 428, 433 (1997) ("Where there is one statute dealing with a subject in general and comprehensive terms, and another dealing with a part of the same subject in a more minute and definite way, the two should be read together and harmonized . . .; but, to the extent of any necessary repugnancy between them, the special statute . . . will prevail over the general statute. . . ."). *See also* Durham Land Owners Ass'n v. Cnty. of Durham, 630 S.E.2d 200, 203, 177 N.C. App. 629, 634 (2006) (reasoning that the call for broad construction under G.S. 153A-4 remains idle when a more specific statute is clear on its face); Bell, note 6 above, at 6 ("[I]n some cases other articles of Chapters 153A and 160A provide such detailed or different requirements for particular kinds of ordinances that it is clear that those procedures must be followed when cities and counties take the actions covered by those specific statutes."). Examples of such specific grants of authority include hearing requirements in planning and development regulations and procedures for disposal of junked or abandoned motor vehicles. *Id.* ("[W]hile in theory local officials can control the disposal of junked or abandoned motor vehicles through either the general police power of G.S. 153A-121(a) and G.S. 160A-174(a) . . . Since the legislature has provided specific rules in these statutes for junked or abandoned vehicle disposal, it is common practice for most officials to 'play it safe' and follow the guidelines."). In the context of school impact fees, the North Carolina Court of Appeals rejected the notion that the general police power provides "an independent source of authority" from the zoning power for a school impact fee and declared that a local government's authority in this regard is limited to "the tools authorized by the zoning statute." *See* Union Land Owners Ass'n v. Cnty. of Union, ___N.C. App. ___, ___, 689 S.E.2d 504, 506–07 (2009).

70. In cases addressing whether local governments must follow the specific procedures set forth in the minimum housing statutes (as opposed to locally generated procedures), courts have required local governments to follow the minimum housing statutory procedures. *See* Newton v. City of Winston-Salem, 92 N.C. App. 446, 449–50, 374 S.E.2d 488, 490–91 (1988). *See also* Town of Hertford v. Harris, 169 N.C. App. 838, 841, 611 S.E.2d 194, 196 (2005) ("Regardless of the specific wording of the town's ordinance, the town must comply with the statute's requirement [in G.S. 160A-443(6)(c)] that any personal property or appurtenances be salvaged and the proceeds applied to the cost of removal or demolition."); Dean v. City of Charlotte, 168 N.C. App. 728, 609 S.E.2d 498, 2005 WL 465906 at *2 (Mar. 1, 2005) (unpublished opinion).

71. *Newton*, 92 N.C. App. at 449–50, 374 S.E.2d at 490–91 (emphasis added). The word "only" appears in the opinion but not in the statute.

72. 92 N.C. App. at 450, 374 S.E.2d at 491. *See also Dean*, 2005 WL 465906 at *2 (2005) ("The enabling legislation provides that an ordinance adopted by a city to regulate buildings unfit for human habitation must contain certain procedures that the city must follow prior to demolition of a dwelling including providing the owner with notice, a hearing, and a reasonable opportunity to bring his or her dwelling into conformity with the housing code."). This result may not have been intended by the statute's drafters. *Cf.* G.S. 160A-450 ("Nothing in this Part shall be construed to abrogate or impair the powers of the courts or of any department of any city to enforce any provisions of its charter or its ordinances or

regulations, nor to prevent or punish violations thereof; and the powers conferred by this Part shall be in addition and supplemental to the powers conferred by any other law.").

73. *See Newton*, 92 N.C. App. at 451–52, 374 S.E.2d at 491–92 (finding city of Winston-Salem was required to follow the specific notice and service requirements for minimum housing ordinances as set forth in G.S. 160A-443, particularly since "[s]tatutes authorizing service by mail or publication are strictly construed and must be followed with particularity").

74. See note 69 above and accompanying text.

75. *See* TRW Inc. v. Andrews, 534 U.S. 19, 31 (2001) ("It is a cardinal principle of statutory construction that a statute ought, upon the whole, to be so construed that, if it can be prevented, no clause, sentence, or word shall be superfluous, void, or insignificant . . . We are reluctant to treat statutory terms as surplusage in any setting.") (internal quotations and citations omitted); State v. Buckner, 351 N.C. 401, 408, 527 S.E.2d 307, 311 (2000) ("If possible, a statute must be interpreted so as to give meaning to all its provisions."). *See also* Five C's, Inc. v. Cnty. of Pasquotank, 195 N.C. App. 410, 415, 672 S.E.2d 737, 741 (2009) (finding that the broad grant of police power authority in G.S. 153A-4 must remain idle if the provisions of an existing statute are to be given meaning: "A county may not therefore use its broad police powers as a guise to enact zoning regulations for manufactured homes inconsistent with N.C. Gen. Stat. § 160A-383.1.").

76. G.S. 160A-443(3)(a) (emphasis added). Under the minimum housing statutes, a public officer may issue an order "requiring the owner, within the time specified, to repair, alter or improve the dwelling *in order to render it fit for human habitation* . . . ." *Id.* (emphasis added).

77. G.S. 160A-443(3)(a).

78. See notes 33–34 above and accompanying text for a discussion of good-repair regulations.

79. See Chapter 3, note 5 and accompanying text.

# 3
# Minimum Housing Statutes

Chapter 1 describes the various sources of authority for imposing repair and maintenance requirements on deteriorating dwellings. It concludes that two sources of authority—the general police power and the minimum housing statutes—are best suited for regulating dwellings prior to the point they deteriorate beyond repair. Chapter 2 focuses on the general police power, the primary source of authority for imposing repair and maintenance requirements on green and yellow condition dwellings. The general police power can also be employed to regulate red condition dwellings, but as Chapter 2 notes, it cannot encroach upon the regulatory scope of the minimum housing statutes. The minimum housing statutes operate in their own exclusive space, and good-repair regulations under the general police power can be used only outside of that space.

This chapter describes the scope of the minimum housing statutes.[1] Section 3.1 discusses the operation and enforcement of local ordinances enacted pursuant to the state's minimum housing statutes. Section 3.2 describes sources of funding for enforcement and other activities undertaken pursuant to the minimum housing statutes. Finally, Section 3.3 discusses local government authority to manipulate certain definitions within a minimum housing ordinance and analyzes the effects of such modifications.

## 3.1 Basic Operation and Enforcement of Minimum Housing Ordinances

North Carolina's minimum housing statutes provide authority for local governments to regulate red condition dwellings—specifically, to require that these unfit dwellings be rendered "fit for human habitation."[2] A city's authority under the statutes extends into its extraterritorial jurisdiction, but a county may exercise its authority within the corporate limits of a city only with that city's permission.[3]

The minimum housing statutes define a dwelling as "unfit for human habitation" when it suffers from defective conditions such as "defects therein increasing the hazards of fire, accident, or other calamities; lack of adequate ventilation, light, or sanitary facilities; dilapidation; disrepair; structural defects; uncleanliness" which render it "dangerous or injurious to the health, safety or morals of the occupants of the dwelling, the occupants of neighboring dwellings, or other residents of the city."[4] This language, which uses words like "dangerous or injurious," "calamities," and "dilapidation," emphasizes the rather extreme character of unfit dwellings. This terminology could be somewhat confining—perhaps restricting the application of minimum housing standards only to dwellings in extremely bad condition—were it not for some additional discretionary language. By statute, local governments are authorized to provide additional standards in an ordinance to guide public officers with respect to how "unfit for human habitation" is defined locally.[5] This discretion is important and will be explored in more detail below.[6] But first, a description of the basic operation of the minimum housing statutes is in order.

As a threshold matter, authority under the minimum housing statutes lies dormant until a local government enacts a minimum housing ordinance.[7] After enacting such an ordinance, the governing body must prepare an estimate of the annual administrative costs of the ordinance, including the costs of equipment, personnel, and supplies.[8] The ordinance must include certain provisions.[9] For example, by statute, all ordinances must designate a public officer to exercise the statutorily prescribed powers.[10] Additionally, all local ordinances must include uniform procedures to be employed when a repair or other corrective action is ordered for a substandard dwelling.[11] The required procedures are set forth in the statute and discussed below. A summary of the procedures is provided as a flowchart in Appendix 1.

### Preliminary Investigation

The appointed public officer must conduct a preliminary investigation into a dwelling's condition either (1) when it appears to the officer that a dwelling is unfit for human habitation or (2) upon receipt of a petition filed by at least five citizens (or by a public authority) charging that a dwelling is unfit for human habitation.[12] Local governments may grant their public officers "any powers necessary or convenient" to perform their investigative and other duties, including the authority to (1) administer oaths or affirmations, examine witnesses, and receive evidence and (2) appoint—and delegate their duties to—other officers, agents, and employees. [13]

The local ordinance may authorize the officer to enter dwellings to investigate in a manner that "will do the least possible inconvenience to the persons in possession,"[14] but the Fourth Amendment to the U.S. Constitution probably restricts this authority.[15] Under the Fourth Amendment, an officer may undertake only investigations that do not violate a person's reasonable expectation of privacy. Examples of proper investigations include viewing the dwelling from a public space[16] or approaching the front door of the residence.[17] With respect to entering a dwelling to conduct administrative inspections and searches of private residences, the United States Supreme Court has ruled that the Fourth Amendment requires public officials to obtain a warrant unless the owner or possessor consents to the entry[18] or an emergency exists.[19] The North Carolina General Statutes provide for the issuance of administrative search warrants in Section 15-27.2. A copy of the form that can be used to request an administrative inspection warrant (and the affidavit supporting the warrant request) is included in Appendix 2.

## Notice and Hearing Requirements

If the officer's preliminary investigation discloses a basis for charges that a dwelling is unfit for human habitation, then the officer "shall" issue a complaint setting forth those charges.[20] The officer shall cause to be served upon the owner and any parties in interest (1) the aforementioned complaint stating the charges and (2) notice of a hearing before the public officer (or the agent of the officer) in the county where the property is located.[21]

### Identification of Those to Be Served

The public officer must first identify the owners and parties in interest of the property who are entitled to service.[22] The statute defines *owner* as the "holder of the title in fee simple and every mortgagee *of record.*"[23] *Parties in interest* are defined as "all individuals, associations and corporations who have interests *of record* in a dwelling and any who are in possession thereof."[24] Thus, under the statute's plain language, a local government need identify only parties with interests of record. However, if the public officer is notified of the existence of parties with unrecorded interests in the property, case law suggests that the officer should act reasonably on that information.[25] Case law is not entirely clear on what acting reasonably entails, but a safe course would be for the officer to provide duplicate notice to those additional parties.[26]

### Service of Complaints and Orders

The statute sets forth detailed requirements for the service of complaints and orders.[27] These service requirements will be strictly construed by a court and must be followed with particularity.[28] Complaints and orders must be served either personally or by registered or certified mail.[29] When service is made by registered or certified mail, a copy may also be sent by regular mail.[30] If a copy is sent by regular mail, a notice of the pending proceedings must be posted in a conspicuous place on the affected premises. Service will be deemed sufficient if the registered or certified mail is unclaimed or refused but the regular mail is not returned by the post office within ten days.[31]

Service by publication (for example, in a newspaper) is available in only two specific circumstances: (1) "[i]f the identities . . . or the whereabouts of persons are unknown" and "cannot be ascertained by the public officer in the exercise of reasonable diligence"[32] or (2) "if the owners are known but have refused to accept service by registered or certified mail."[33] To effectuate service by publication, the public officer must first make an affidavit certifying that either of the two prior circumstances exists. Then, service may be completed by (1) publishing notice in a newspaper of general circulation in the city,[34] (2) publishing notice at least once no later than the time in which personal service would be required under the statute, and (3) posting notice of the pending proceedings in a conspicuous place on the premises affected.[35]

For example, say that a public officer sends to an owner via registered mail a complaint and notice of hearing regarding a dwelling's unfitness for human habitation. The registered mail is returned with an endorsement or stamp noting "Refused." The public officer may now make an affidavit certifying that service has been refused, allowing service to be completed by publication. The statutory time requirement for personal service of the complaint and notice of hearing is at least ten days and no more than thirty days before the hearing date fixed in the complaint.[36] Therefore, for proper service by publication, the notice must be published in a newspaper of general circulation in the city or county in which the dwelling is located within this same time frame—that is, at least ten days and no more than thirty days before the hearing date.[37] The public officer must also post notice of the pending proceedings in a conspicuous place on the dwelling itself.[38]

### Hearing

As already noted, the hearing on whether a dwelling is unfit for human habitation must take place not less than ten days and not more than thirty days after service of the complaint.[39] The hearing is held before the public officer or the officer's designated agent.[40] Both the owner and the parties in interest have the right to (1) file an answer to the complaint and (2) appear in person or otherwise give testimony at the hearing.[41] The rules of evidence do not apply at the hearing.[42] If any party is dissatisfied with the public officer's decision, the party may appeal the decision to the appropriate board.[43]

### *Standard of Strict Compliance*

Local governments may be liable for damages resulting from a failure to comply with the specific statutory notice and hearing requirements.[44] Strict compliance requires the public officer to adhere to all of the statutory notice procedures even when the property owner has otherwise received actual notice.[45] When the character of the local government's action changes—for instance, when an order to repair is replaced with an order to demolish— the change involves a "different determination" and entitles the property owner to a new notice and hearing.[46]

## Orders and Enforcement under Minimum Housing Ordinances

Once a public officer has properly convened a hearing and determined that a dwelling is unfit for human habitation, the officer is required to take action. The public officer, after making written findings of fact, "shall issue" one of two possible orders to the property owner: an order to "remove or demolish" or an order to "repair."[47] The order to be issued depends on whether the dwelling can be repaired at reasonable cost. Local governments are explicitly authorized to define in their ordinances what percentage of a dwelling's value constitutes a reasonable cost for repair.[48] Once the appropriate order to be issued has been determined, the public officer must serve the order in accordance with the same service requirements described above for complaints.[49]

### *Order to Remove or Demolish*

If the cost of repair exceeds the "reasonable cost" in relation to the value of the dwelling, the public officer "shall" issue and serve upon the owner an order requiring the property owner to remove or demolish the dwelling.[50] Note that there is no option to order the repair of the dwelling. Because case law suggests that unfit dwellings may be regulated only in the manner provided by the minimum housing statutes,[51] the public officer may not order repair once the cost of repair exceeds the defined reasonable cost. However, practically speaking, repair by the owner would probably end the matter. Additionally, if any affordable housing organizations have filed a written request to receive notices of orders to remove or demolish, the public officer must notify them via first-class mail.[52] Demolition by action of the public officer may not proceed until forty-five days after mailing these notices.

If the property owner fails to comply with the order to remove or demolish, the local government may effectuate the order, but only after the property owner has "first been given a reasonable opportunity to bring [the dwelling] into conformity with housing codes."[53] Then, to effectuate the order, the governing body must adopt an *ordinance* which describes the particular property in question and directs the public officer to remove or demolish the dwelling.[54] Adopting an ordinance requires holding a public hearing prior to adoption in compliance with G.S. 160A-364 (for cities) and G.S. 153A-323 (counties).[55] This ordinance must be recorded and indexed in the name of the property owner in the office of the register of deeds.[56] Following recordation and the expiration of the forty-five day wait period mentioned above, the public officer may proceed to remove or demolish the dwelling.

Recoupment of the costs of demolition requires strict adherence to a two-step statutory procedure: (1) sell the "materials of the dwelling and any personal property, fixtures, or appurtenances found in or attached to the dwelling" and (2) apply those proceeds to the cost of removal or demolition.[57] No deviation is permitted, regardless of the wording of a local government's specific ordinance.[58] Any proceeds remaining after the removal or demolition must be deposited in superior court and disbursed as the court directs.[59] If the proceeds of the sale are insufficient to cover the costs of removal or demolition, the remaining costs become a lien on the property, which is collected as a lien for a special assessment.[60] This lien is described below in Section 3.2.

### Order to Repair

If the dwelling can be repaired at "reasonable cost in relation to the value of the dwelling," the public officer "shall" issue and serve upon the owner an order requiring the property owner to "repair, alter or improve the dwelling in order to render it fit for human habitation."[61] When the officer issues an order to repair, he or she may also issue an order to vacate and close the dwelling, but only if "continued occupancy during the time allowed for repair will present a significant threat of bodily harm."[62] The phrase "during the time allowed for repair" suggests the drafters intended the vacate and close order to be temporary, lasting only until the ordered repairs are complete. Upon issuance of a vacate and close order, the public officer must also notify via first-class mail any affordable housing organizations that have requested to be notified of vacate and close determinations.[63]

If the property owner fails to make the repairs within the time allotted in the order, the local government may respond in one of two ways: it may (1) "cause the dwelling to be repaired, altered or improved," essentially effectuating the repair order or (2) cause the dwelling to be vacated and closed without effectuating the repair order.[64]

To proceed with the repair option, as seen with demolition,[65] the governing body must first adopt an *ordinance* describing the particular property and ordering the public officer to effectuate the repair.[66] Prior to adoption of this ordinance, a public hearing must be held in compliance with G.S. 160A-364 (cities) and G.S. 153A-323 (counties).[67] The ordinance must be recorded and indexed in the name of the property owner in the office of the register of deeds.[68] Here, as with effectuation of an order to demolish, the costs of effectuation become a lien on the property, which is collected as a lien for a special assessment.[69]

Vacating and closing the dwelling involves similar steps with a few additional considerations. An ordinance must be enacted that directs the public officer to vacate and close the dwelling. Prior to enactment, a public hearing must be held pursuant to G.S 160A-364 or G.S. 153A-323. Following enactment, the ordinance must be recorded and indexed in the name of the property owner. In keeping with the original intent of the statute— although no longer technically required—the public officer should notify affordable housing organizations of any ordinance directing a dwelling to be vacated and closed.[70] Upon recordation of the ordinance, the public officer may immediately proceed to vacate and close the dwelling; no waiting period is required. The costs of vacating and closing the dwelling become a lien on the property that is collected as a lien for a special assessment.[71]

In addition to effectuating the vacate and close order, the public officer may post a notice on any building so closed declaring that the building is unfit for human habitation and that occupation of the building is a Class 1 misdemeanor.[72] The public officer is authorized to enforce compliance against unlawful occupants by filing a civil action in the nature of summary ejectment.[73]

Once a dwelling is vacated and closed in this manner and unless it is subsequently repaired or demolished by the owner, the local government must leave it in its vacated and closed state until (1) the local government itself effectuates the repair before the dwelling deteriorates significantly;[74] (2) the dwelling deteriorates to the point that the cost of repair exceeds a reasonable cost, in which case the local government must start over with new proceedings to obtain an order to demolish the dwelling;[75] or (3) the local government qualifies for and avails itself of the abandonment of intent to repair process, which provides special procedures for repairing or demolishing dwellings that have been vacated and closed for at least one year.[76]

### Abandonment of the Intent to Repair Procedure

Prior to amendments enacted in 2009,[77] the minimum housing statutes required local governments to give every owner of an unfit—but reparable—dwelling a choice whether to repair the structure or to vacate and close it.[78] Not surprisingly, many owners without sufficient resources to repair a dwelling simply opted to vacate and close it, leaving it in its unfit state. When those vacated and closed dwellings became blighting influences in the community, a local government had no recourse but to wait until the dwelling deteriorated to the point that it became eligible for demolition. This result was untenable to many local governments.

To address this specific problem, a remedy was developed and is available to municipalities in counties with populations of over 71,000,[79] municipalities with populations exceeding 190,000,[80] and certain enumerated smaller municipalities.[81] When one of these eligible local governments finds that a property owner has "abandoned the intent and purpose to repair" by keeping a dwelling vacated and closed for one year pursuant to an order to vacate and close, and certain other findings are made about the dwelling's blighting influence,[82] the local government may enact one of two ordinances and serve it upon the owner.[83] The first ordinance, applicable only if repairs can be made at a cost not exceeding 50 percent of the "then current value of the dwelling," is an order to "either *repair* or *demolish and remove* the dwelling within 90 days."[84] The second ordinance, applicable if repair costs would exceed the 50 percent threshold described above, orders the owner to "demolish and remove the dwelling within 90 days."[85] If an owner fails to comply with whichever order is issued, the appointed public officer "shall effectuate" the order, with the costs becoming a lien on the property and collected as a special assessment.[86]

These procedures presumably are also available to eligible local governments when a vacate and close order is issued only as a temporary measure for the protection of residents during the time allowed for repair.[87] Recall that this temporary order to vacate and close is issued in conjunction with a repair order. If an owner fails to comply with the repair order, the public officer is authorized to cause the dwelling to be repaired or vacated and closed.[88]

But what if the public officer responds to the owner's noncompliance by taking no action at all and the dwelling simply continues under the temporary vacate and close order without being repaired? After a dwelling has been vacated and closed one year without any repair activity, eligible local governments may utilize the abandonment of intent to repair procedures for a temporarily closed dwelling just as they would for a permanently closed dwelling.[89] Accordingly, for a temporarily vacated and closed dwelling, local governments may choose from the same three options they have following issuance of a permanent vacate and close order. That is, a temporarily closed dwelling, unless sooner repaired or demolished by the owner, remains closed until (1) the local government effectuates the repair itself; (2) the dwelling deteriorates to the point that the cost of repair exceeds a reasonable cost, in which case the local government must initiate new proceedings to obtain an order to demolish the dwelling; or (3) the local government qualifies for and avails itself of the abandonment of intent to repair procedures.[90]

Occasionally an owner may make a meager attempt at repairs but fail to complete them within one year following issuance of a temporary vacate and close order. In that case, an eligible local government may still avail itself of the abandonment of intent to repair procedures, but only if the government finds that the owner has in fact abandoned the intent to repair.[91] If, however, repair activity has commenced and is being meaningfully pursued, the abandonment of intent to repair procedures may not be used. Meaningful repair activity would indicate that the owner has not abandoned the "intent and purpose to repair."[92]

### Effectuation of a Repair Order over One Year Old

The statute imposes no time limit on a local government's ability to effectuate a repair order, but the effective duration of any repair order is likely limited by reasonableness and due process considerations.[93] In any event, prior to effectuating an old repair order, a local government should reinspect the affected property to determine whether there have been any developments that might halt local government effectuation, such as a change in the condition of the property[94] or the initiation of repairs by the owners.[95]

### Appeals Board

A local government may—but is not required to—establish a housing appeals board to which any appeals of the public officer's decisions or orders are made.[96] The composition and powers of a housing appeals board are set by statute.[97] Alternatively, a local government may choose to have such appeals heard by its zoning board of adjustment.[98] Regardless of which board is assigned this function, property owners disputing their treatment under a minimum housing ordinance must exhaust the local government's appeal process prior to resorting to the courts.[99]

The appeals board possesses all powers of the public officer—and thus may affirm or modify any order—but a concurring vote of four of the five board members is required to reverse or modify any decision or order of the public officer.[100] By statute zoning boards of adjustment are composed of at least five members,[101] and the four-fifths majority rule used for those boards would be analogous to the voting requirement for appeals boards and should be applied when a zoning board of adjustment serves as the appeals board.[102] The appeals board is granted discretion to interpret ordinances and adapt the "strict letter of the ordinance" to the facts of any given case, but it must observe the "spirit of the ordinance" while pursuing public safety, public welfare, and substantial justice.[103]

To initiate an appeal of the decision or order of a public officer, an aggrieved party must file a notice of appeal with both the public officer and the board, specifying the grounds upon which the appeal is based.[104] The notice of appeal must be filed within ten days of the public officer's decision or order.[105] Upon the filing of an appeal, the public officer transmits to the board all records on which the public officer's decision or order was based.[106] The appeal suspends any requirement of action the order requires, unless the public officer certifies to the board that the suspension would cause imminent peril to life or property (in which case the requirement will not be suspended except by restraining order).[107] If the appeal is from a decision refusing to allow the aggrieved party to act, the decision will remain in force until modified or reversed.[108]

Once the board renders a decision, the courts provide the next level of review. A request for court review must be instituted within fifteen days of the board's decision.[109] An aggrieved party may also, within thirty days of the board's decision, petition the superior court for an injunction preventing the public officer from carrying out the board's order or decision until a final disposition of the case.[110] Hearings on such a petition must be held within twenty days and will be given preference on the court's calendar.[111]

## 3.2 Recoupment of Costs for Minimum Housing Activities

Upon initial enactment of a minimum housing ordinance, the governing body must prepare an estimate of the annual cost of administering the ordinance, including the costs of necessary equipment, personnel, and supplies.[112] These costs may be paid by making appropriations from the local government's "revenues"—though probably not from revenues statutorily earmarked for other purposes—and by grants or donations.[113] Recoupment of costs related to minimum housing activities is obtained primarily from two sources: liens and fees. Fines and civil penalties are probably not authorized for the reasons discussed below.

### Liens

The cost of effectuating an order pursuant to a minimum housing ordinance may be recouped from the owner. The costs associated with effectuation become a lien on the affected property and are collected as a lien for a special assessment.[114] Special assessment liens hold virtually the same priority as property tax liens.[115] The collection methods available for minimum housing liens are therefore more robust[116] than for mechanics liens (the lien available for police power regulations). Furthermore, special assessment liens survive foreclosure, whereas mechanics liens generally do not.[117]

For costs incurred to repair or demolish a dwelling in an incorporated city, the minimum housing statutes provide for an additional lien on the owner's other real property—except the owner's primary residence—located within the city limits or within one mile of the city limits.[118] This supplementary lien is inferior to all prior liens on a parcel and is collectable only as a money judgment.[119]

### Fees

The *Homebuilders* case stands for the proposition that North Carolina local governments are authorized to assess reasonable fees to cover the costs of regulatory activities undertaken pursuant to express statutory authority.[120] Such authority certainly exists in the case of minimum housing activities, but other case law leaves some doubt about whether fees are permissible in the context of minimum housing regulations. The concern stems from a Court of Appeals interpretation of the minimum housing statutes in *Newton v. City of Winston-Salem,* that the power to regulate unfit dwellings may be exercised only in the manner provided by the minimum housing statutes.[121] These statutes make no mention of fees. The only funding sources enumerated within the statutes are those discussed above: appropriations from local government revenues generally[122] and liens for recoupment of costs associated with effectuating orders.[123] However, the court in *Homebuilders* found *implied* authority for fees even in the absence of *express* authority for them. The only express authority required by *Homebuilders* is the authority to conduct the underlying regulatory activity, which is precisely the situation presented by the minimum housing statutes. Accordingly, the establishment of a reasonable fee schedule designed to cover only the costs of administering the minimum housing program is probably permissible.

### Fines and Civil Penalties

*Newton*'s strict interpretation of the minimum housing statutes raises a similar issue with respect to fines and civil penalties. The minimum housing statutes provide no authority for local governments to assess fines or civil penalties to enforce orders issued under the statutes, except in the specific case of unlawful occupation of a closed dwelling.[124] A local government would therefore need to rely on its general authority to impose fines or penalties for enforcement of ordinances.[125] Since *Newton* indicates that unfit dwellings may be regulated only in the manner provided by the minimum housing statutes,[126] the question arises whether a local government can use its general authority to impose fines and penalties for minimum housing enforcement.

Applying a rule of statutory interpretation provides the answer. Fines and civil penalties imposed to enforce orders issued under a minimum housing ordinance would actually be repugnant to the procedural protections afforded to owners by the minimum housing statutes.[127] These protections—such as notice, hearings, required findings, and wait periods prior to effectuation under abandonment of intent to repair procedures—would essentially be eviscerated if, for example, a local government imposed a fine for each day's continuing violation of an order to repair.[128] It must be concluded, therefore, that the general authority to impose fines and civil penalties cannot be employed to enforce minimum housing orders.

## 3.3 Manipulation of Minimum Housing Ordinance Definitions

The minimum housing statutes grant local governments authority to modify two important parameters in minimum housing ordinances: (1) "reasonable cost," which is the percentage of a dwelling's value that determines the order to be issued by the local government (either "remove or demolish" or "repair") and (2) "additional standards" to guide public officers with respect to the definition of "unfit for human habitation." What is the effect of modifying these parameters in local ordinances?

## Reasonable Cost Percentage

Adjustments to the reasonable cost threshold affect the point at which a dwelling's deterioration can no longer be addressed by an order to repair and instead an order to remove or demolish is required. For example, a local government could lower its reasonable cost threshold to 20 percent. In this example, once the cost of repairing a dwelling exceeds 20 percent of its current value, by statute the only order available to the local government is an order for the dwelling's demolition.[129] This low reasonable cost threshold narrows the availability of the repair option and hastens the arrival of the moment at which the remove or demolish order must be applied to a troubled property. Say that the public officer in this hypothetical jurisdiction determines that the cost of repairing an unfit dwelling would be 25 percent of its current value, thereby exceeding the 20 percent threshold. This dwelling might not be terribly dilapidated and therefore might be a good candidate for repair and preservation, yet an order to repair would not be an option. The local government would only be authorized to order that the dwelling be removed or demolished.

We would thus expect a lower reasonable cost threshold to result in more demolition orders and hence more demolitions. This option might appeal to a local government facing a shrinking populace and seeking to eliminate excess housing capacity. However, most North Carolina cities and counties are encountering the opposite problem. The U.S. Census Bureau has forecast that North Carolina's population will increase by more than four million people between 2000 and 2030,[130] so North Carolina local governments would be expected to embark on housing preservation initiatives rather than demolition programs. A higher threshold would be more consistent with preservation efforts because it would lead to a greater number of initial orders to repair rather than to remove or demolish.

## Additional Standards for Defining *Unfit for Human Habitation*

The minimum housing statutes permit local governments to provide additional standards in their minimum housing ordinances to guide public officers with respect to the definition of *unfit for human habitation*, producing two primary consequences.[131] First, this flexibility may lead to confusion about the regulatory coverage of the general police power as compared with the minimum housing statutes, simply because the definition of unfit for human habitation plays a substantial role in determining which of these two schemes will be used to regulate a particular dwelling component.[132] Second, this flexibility provides a local government with an opportunity to expand or contract the reach of its local minimum housing ordinance according to its preference. On one hand, the flexibility is beneficial because it permits a local government to customize its response to substandard housing. On the other, it may tempt a local government to expand the coverage of its ordinance, for example, to conditions that might not actually meet the standard of unfit for human habitation as that term is statutorily defined. If too far-reaching, such expansion could invite claims that the ordinance exceeds the local government's authority under the minimum housing statutes.

The point can be illustrated by describing the effects of a hypothetical municipality's additional standards pertaining to the definition of unfit for human habitation. Consider the following definition.

> A dwelling shall be unfit for human habitation if it fails to meet one or more of the following standards:
>
> 1. There is no deterioration due to the elements because of a lack of preventive maintenance such as painting, waterproofing, and repair.
> 2. Windows shall have panes without cracks or holes.
> 3. Accessory buildings are maintained in a state of good repair.
> 4. Driveways and sidewalks are maintained in good repair.
> 5. Combustible and noncombustible rubbish is removed from the premises.[133]

Some may view these standards, which can be found in a handful of North Carolina local ordinances, as surprisingly broad. A public officer could conceivably declare a dwelling exhibiting any of these conditions as unfit for human habitation; that is, for having a cracked window pane; or perhaps a lightly deteriorated panel on its exterior due to worn paint; or perhaps an accessory building found in disrepair, even though the building is not used for human habitation. Although these standards stretch a reasonable interpretation of the definition of unfit for human habitation, we cannot say for certain they are overbroad; no judicial precedent clarifies at what point a minimum housing ordinance exceeds its statutory authority by applying an overly expansive definition of unfit for human habitation.

The effect of manipulating additional standards must also be understood with respect to the dividing line between the applicability of the general police power versus that of the minimum housing statutes. The sample standards listed above expand the scope of the local government's minimum housing ordinance to a broader set of conditions that might not be considered unfit in another locality. This expansion simultaneously diminishes the reach of regulations derived from the general police power. As discussed in Section 2.5, substandard conditions determinative of a dwelling's fitness or unfitness for human habitation cannot be regulated using the general police power; they may be regulated only pursuant to the minimum housing statutes. Some local governments might view this expansion of minimum housing authority at the expense of police power regulations as a desirable result—particularly those that prefer to regulate substandard dwellings using the minimum housing statutes rather than the general police power.

The trade-offs are worth considering. Minimum housing ordinances have several advantages: the statutory procedures are already established, some case law exists, a city can employ its minimum housing ordinance in its extraterritorial jurisdiction, notice requirements are clearly enumerated, hearings are administrative in nature rather than judicial,[134] and any costs incurred to effectuate orders following noncompliance become a high-priority lien.[135] On the other hand, the general police power has some appeal of its own: it can be used to seamlessly regulate aesthetic and non-aesthetic conditions at an early stage before a dwelling becomes unfit for human habitation, the ability to levy fines or civil penalties may be a powerful tool,[136] and the absence of an existing regulatory scheme and procedures allows for some creativity in design and implementation of local regulations. In addition, jurisdictions with limited resources and ineligible to use the abandonment of intent to repair procedure may have difficulty using the minimum housing statutes to regulate dwellings.

Despite any comparative advantage one type of authority may have over the other, a local government seeking a comprehensive approach to repair-oriented code enforcement does not face an "either-or" choice. Rather, in constructing a comprehensive regulatory program, a local government must rely upon its authority under both the minimum housing statutes and the general police power. The need to use both authorities produces some interesting and difficult challenges as presented in the next chapter.

## Notes

1. See Chapter 2, note 76 and accompanying text.
2. The minimum housing statutes were most recently modified during the 2009 session of the General Assembly. S.L. 2009-279, sec. 7, N.C. Gen. Stat. (hereinafter G.S.) § 160A-443(3).
3. *See* G.S. 160A-360; G.S. 160A-441.

4. G.S. 160A-444. See also G.S. 160A-441, which uses slightly different language to define *unfit for human habitation*, referring, for example, to conditions "dangerous or detrimental" rather than "dangerous or injurious."

5. G.S. 160A-444 ("The ordinances [adopted by a city under this Part] may provide additional standards to guide the public officers, or his agents, in determining the fitness of a dwelling for human habitation.").

6. The power to manipulate the definition of *unfit for human habitation* and the possible consequences of doing so is discussed in Section 3.3.

7. G.S. 160A-443 ("Upon the adoption of an ordinance finding that dwelling conditions of the character described in G.S. 160A-441 exist within a city, the governing body of the city is hereby authorized to adopt and enforce ordinances relating to dwellings within the city's territorial jurisdiction that are unfit for human habitation."). A municipality's territorial jurisdiction for purposes of the minimum housing code is defined by G.S. 160A-360 to include its extraterritorial jurisdiction. Therefore, a municipality can enforce its minimum housing code in its extraterritorial jurisdiction. Compare this with the general police power. A municipality generally cannot exercise its police power within its extraterritorial jurisdiction. (A notable exception to the territorial limits of the general police power is for the abatement of public health nuisances pursuant to G.S. 160A-193, which permits such abatement within one mile of the city limits irrespective of the boundaries of the extraterritorial jurisdiction.)

8. G.S. 160A-449.

9. G.S. 160A-443 ("These ordinances *shall include* the following provisions . . . ." (emphasis added)). The precise and detailed nature of some of the statutory requirements can be illustrated by the requirements pertaining to heat sources. Cities with a population of 200,000 or more must require dwellings leased as rental properties to have a heat source sufficient to heat at least one habitable room (excluding the kitchen) to a minimum temperature of 68 degrees, measured 3 feet above the floor, when the outside temperature is 20 degrees Fahrenheit. G.S. 160A-443.1.

10. G.S. 160A-443(1). *See also* G.S. 160A-448 ("An ordinance adopted by the governing body of the city may authorize the public officer to exercise any powers necessary or convenient to carry out and effectuate the purpose and provisions of this Part, including the following powers . . . (1) To investigate the dwelling conditions in the city . . . (2) To administer oaths, affirmations, examine witnesses and receive evidence; (3) To enter upon premises for the purpose of making examinations in a manner that will do the least possible inconvenience to the persons in possession; (4) To appoint and fix the duties of officers, agents and employees necessary to carry out the purposes of the ordinances; and (5) To delegate any of his functions and powers. . .").

11. These procedures were most recently modified by amendments that became effective October 1, 2009. *See* S.L. 2009-279.

12. G.S. 160A-443(2). A local government, pursuant to G.S. 160A-448, may authorize its appointed minimum housing public officer to exercise powers such as entering upon premises to examine dwellings. A reasonable statutory interpretation argument can be made that this authority of the appointed public officer is distinct from the authority granted to inspections departments by G.S. 160A-424 and G.S. 153A-364. It is uncertain how a court would treat this argument, but assuming the distinction is correct, it follows that restrictions imposed *specifically on inspection departments* by G.S. 160A-424 and G.S. 153A-364 would not apply to an appointed minimum housing public officer.

13. G.S. 160A-448.

14. *Id.*

15. Wolf v. Colorado, 338 U.S. 25, 27–28 (1949) (holding the Fourth Amendment's prohibition against unreasonable searches and seizures as binding on the states under the due process provisions of the Fourteenth Amendment). For a detailed description of

administrative inspections, including examples of proper and improper inspections and an explanation of the mechanics of an administrative inspection warrant, see DAVID W. OWENS, LAND USE LAW IN NORTH CAROLINA 172–74 (2006).

16. Payton v. New York, 445 U.S. 573 (1980).

17. State v. Tripp, 52 N.C. App. 244, 278 S.E.2d 592 (1981); State v. Prevette, 43 N.C. App. 450, 259 S.E.2d 595 (1979), *review denied,* 299 N.C. 124, 261 S.E.2d 925, *cert. denied,* 447 U.S. 906 (1980). For a more detailed description of administrative inspections, see OWENS, note 15 above.

18. Camara v. Mun. Court of S.F., 387 U.S. 523, 539–40 (1967) ("[M]ost citizens allow inspections of their property without a warrant. Thus, as a practical matter and in light of the Fourth Amendment's requirement that a warrant specify the property to be searched, it seems likely that warrants should normally be sought only after entry is refused unless there has been a citizen complaint or there is other satisfactory reason for securing immediate entry.").

19. *Id.* at 539 ("Since our holding emphasizes the controlling standard of reasonableness, nothing we say today is intended to foreclose prompt inspections, even without a warrant, that the law has traditionally upheld in emergency situations.") (citing N. Am. Cold Storage Co. v. City of Chicago, 211 U.S. 306 (1908) (seizure of unwholesome food); Jacobson v. Massachusetts, 197 U.S. 11 (1905) (compulsory smallpox vaccination); Compagnie Francaise v. Bd. of Health, 186 U.S. 380 (1902) (health quarantine); Kroplin v. Truax, 165 N.E. 498 (Ohio St. 1929) (summary destruction of tubercular cattle)).

20. G.S. 160A-443(2).

21. *Id.*

22. As a way of dealing with absentee property owners, several jurisdictions—including Winston-Salem, Gastonia, Durham, and Cumberland County—have sought and received special authority from the General Assembly to require nonresident owners of rental property to designate a local resident to serve as the agent for receipt of notice of housing code violations.

23. G.S. 160A-442(4) (emphasis added).

24. G.S. 160A-442(5) (emphasis added). *See also* Mennonite Bd. of Missions v. Adams, 462 U.S. 791, 103 S. Ct. 2706 (1983) (concluding that, for proceedings in which property interests of a mortgagee could be adversely affected, notice to mortgagor was insufficient and instead notice by mail to ensure personal service was the minimum required to any party whose property interests would be adversely affected, provided that names and addresses are reasonably attainable).

25. *See* Lawyer v. City of Elizabeth City, 199 N.C. App. 304, 308–09, 681 S.E.2d 415, 418 (2009). In *Lawyer,* the public officer relied on assurances from the city's tax department and register of deeds that the owners of record had been identified. However, the plaintiffs had not been identified as owners. Plaintiffs had purchased the property at a sheriff's sale and had notified the city's tax department by letter of their purchase—even requesting that tax bills be forwarded to them—but had failed to record their deed. The plaintiffs were therefore owners, but not owners of record. In an opinion that omitted any discussion of the plain language of the statute and the importance of recordation under North Carolina law, the appeals court sent the case back to the trial court to determine whether the public officer should nonetheless have conducted a more diligent search to identify the existence of the unrecorded deed from the sheriff's sale. The court opined that reasonable minds could differ as to whether the public officer should have taken additional steps to identify the unrecorded deed.

26. *Id.* The court appeared to back away from creating a new reasonableness requirement when it concluded, "However, it is not clear that the City was required to [take additional steps] in this circumstance. The extent of its duty may have been for [the public officer] to do exactly as he did." Thus, public officers are not necessarily required to conduct a full title search to determine the identity of owners without recorded interests, but if a public officer receives notice of the existence of an unrecorded deed, the officer should provide duplicate

notice of any minimum housing proceedings to the owners of such unrecorded interests.

27. *See* G.S. 160A-445.

28. Newton v. City of Winston-Salem, 92 N.C. App. 446, 452, 374 S.E.2d 488, 492 (1988) ("Statutes authorizing service by mail or publication are strictly construed and must be followed with particularity.") (citing Hassell v. Wilson, 301 N.C. 307, 314, 272 S.E.2d 77, 82 (1980)).

29. G.S. 160A-445.

30. *Id.*

31. *Id.*

32. When a question arises as to whether a public officer exercised reasonable diligence in identifying interested parties and ascertaining their whereabouts as required prior to using service by publication under G.S. 160A-445, courts have required a factual inquiry at the trial court level and will not grant summary judgment in favor of either party. *See* Farmers Bank of Sunbury v. City of Elizabeth City, 54 N.C. App. 110, 282 S.E.2d 580 (1981) (noting that summary judgment is inappropriate when the question involves the reasonableness of the actions of the party requesting summary judgment and reversing summary judgment for city when the only evidence advanced by the city that its public officer exercised the statutorily required reasonable diligence was the assertion to that effect in the officer's affidavit).

33. G.S. 160A-445(a1). Refusal of service cannot be inferred if registered or certified mail is returned "unclaimed." *Newton*, 92 N.C. App. at 452, 374 S.E.2d at 492. Note that this clause permits service by publication only when the "owners" are known but refuse service. The statute is unclear on how to proceed if persons other than the owners are known but refuse service by registered or certified mail (unless a copy was also sent by regular mail and is not returned by the post office). It would appear at first glance that personal service is the only available option for a non-owner that has refused service. Contrast that result with the fact that owners in the same position can be served through publication. If this difference in treatment was intended, it is an odd result that offers non-owners greater procedural protection than owners. However, it was probably not intended by the statute's drafters. The statute specifically allows that service "upon the owners *or other persons* may be made by publication," so presumably, authority to conduct service by publication is triggered when either an owner or non-owner refuses service by registered or certified mail.

34. The definition of *city* in G.S. 160A-442 includes any county. *See* G.S. 160A-442(1) ("'City' means any incorporated city or any county.").

35. G.S. 160A-445(a1).

36. *See* G.S. 160A-443(2) ("a hearing will be held before the public officer (or his designated agent) at a place within the county in which the property is located fixed not less than 10 days nor more than 30 days after the serving of the complaint").

37. See notes 35 and 36 above and accompanying text.

38. *Id.*

39. See note 36 above. Presumably the date of service on the owners—not other parties—controls for this purpose.

40. G.S. 160A-443(2).

41. *Id.*

42. *Id.*

43. The procedures pertaining to appeals of the public officer's decisions are discussed in "Appeals Board," below.

44. Newton v. City of Winston-Salem, 92 N.C. App. 446, 452, 374 S.E.2d 488, 492 (1988) ("'A municipal corporation is liable for the destruction or demolition of a building as a public nuisance . . . where the City did not observe due process requirements.' The City acted at its peril in failing to exercise its powers in the manner prescribed by the statute, and thus it is liable to plaintiff for any provable damages.") (quoting McQuillin, *Municipal Corporations,* § 24-561).

45. *Newton,* 92 N.C. App. at 452–53, 374 S.E.2d at 492 ("Statutes authorizing service by mail or publication are strictly construed and must be followed with particularity . . . . 'Actual notice, given in any manner other than that prescribed by statute cannot supply constitutional validity to the statute or to service under it.' . . . The trial court erred in instructing the jury that it could find that the defendant used reasonable diligence to provide actual notice and thus absolve the defendant of its liability for damages to plaintiff, even though the defendant failed to serve the plaintiff as required by law before demolishing the building.") (quoting Distribs., Inc. v. McAndrews, 270 N.C. 91, 94, 153 S.E.2d 770, 772 (1967)).

46. *Newton,* 92 N.C. App. at 451–52, 374 S.E.2d at 492 ("An order to repair is issued after a determination that repairs can be made at a reasonable cost in relation to the value of the dwelling. An order to demolish involves a different determination, namely, that the repairs *cannot* be made at a reasonable cost in relation to the value of the dwelling. These are clearly two distinct factual determinations supporting two distinct kinds of orders. In this case, the City's demolition order was issued almost three years after the City held a hearing and issued its order to repair. The demolition order was based on the building inspector's determination that 'the condition of the property had changed' due to vandalism. Plaintiff was given no opportunity to be heard on this determination as required by § 160A- 443(3). . . The City acted without authority in ordering the demolition of plaintiff's building without affording plaintiff notice and an opportunity to be heard as required by statute").

47. G.S. 160A-443(3)a. The compulsory nature of some aspects of the minimum housing statutes—in this case, requiring the public officer to proceed with issuing an order of some kind—may trouble some local governing boards, particularly given the fact that the public officer's investigation can be triggered by as few as five complaining citizens. This may be one reason that several North Carolina local governments have declined to enact a minimum housing ordinance. However, without such an ordinance, local government authority to regulate red condition dwellings is very limited, as described in Section 2.5 (discussing how the minimum housing statutes occupy some exclusive regulatory space, thereby limiting the extent to which a local government may utilize its general police power to impose maintenance standards on red condition dwellings).

48. Both G.S. 160A-443(3)a. and b. state that "the ordinance of the city may fix a certain percentage of [the value of the dwelling] as being reasonable." The consequences of manipulating this percentage are discussed in Section 3.3.

49. G.S. 160A-445. These requirements are discussed in "Service of Complaints and Orders," above.

50. G.S. 160A-443(3)b. Service of orders is described in "Service of Complaints and Orders," above.

51. See Chapter 2, notes 71–75 and accompanying text.

52. G.S. 160A-443(8).

53. G.S. 160A-443(5). *See also* Horton v. Gulledge, 277 N.C. 353, 363, 177 S.E.2d 885, 892 (1970) ("In the instant case, it appears from the findings of the Housing Commission that the house in question can be repaired so as to comply with the city's Housing Code, be suitable for human habitation and be no longer a threat to public health, safety, morals or general welfare. To require its destruction, without giving the owner a reasonable opportunity thus to remove the existing threat to the public health, safety and welfare, is arbitrary and unreasonable."). There is little guidance as to what constitutes "reasonable opportunity," but in one condemnation case, forty days following constructive notice to the owner was considered sufficient, when during that time the owner failed to take any action or formulate a plan to restore the building. Coffey v. Town of Waynesville, 143 N.C. App. 624, 634, 547 S.E.2d 132, 139 (2001).

54. G.S. 160A-443(5). To quote the exact language in the statute, the governing body must order the public officer "to proceed to effectuate the purpose of this Article." *Id.* This

precise statutory language would presumably afford the public officer some discretion in deciding exactly how to proceed with effectuation, which might include delaying action in the event the owner agrees to comply with the order voluntarily or makes satisfactory progress in bringing the dwelling into compliance with housing codes. It is nonetheless still consistent with the statute for a governing body to adopt an ordinance directing the officer to effectuate "removal or demolition" specifically, and even under this more specific order, a public officer presumably could still exercise some discretion by delaying action if an owner became compliant.

55. G.S. 160A-364 mandates that a public hearing be held prior to "adopting, amending, or repealing any ordinance authorized by this Article [19 of Chapter 160A]." As the minimum housing statutes are found in Article 19 of Chapter 160A, the adoption of an ordinance directing the demolition of a dwelling triggers the hearing requirement. Notice for the hearing must be (1) given once a week for two successive calendar weeks in a newspaper having general circulation in the area and (2) published the first time not less than ten days nor more than twenty-five days before the date fixed for the hearing, with the day of the hearing but not the day of publication to be included in this computation. G.S. 153A-323 places an identical hearing requirement on counties.

56. G.S. 160A-443(5).

57. G.S. 160A-443(6)c. Procedures for sale are not specified. It would be reasonable for a public officer to utilize the local government's procedures for sale of personal property under G.S. 160A-266, assuming the value of the materials does not exceed the limitations of that statute.

58. Town of Hertford v. Harris, 169 N.C. App. 838, 841, 611 S.E.2d 194, 196 (2005) (finding that summary judgment for the town was not proper when there was a genuine issue of material fact as to whether any salvageable personal property existed in the mobile home that could be applied to the cost of removal or demolition: "Regardless of the specific wording of the town's ordinance, the town must comply with the statute's requirement [in G.S. 160A-443(6)c.] that any personal property or appurtenances be salvaged and the proceeds applied to the cost of removal or demolition.").

59. G.S. 160A-443(6)c.

60. G.S. 160A-443(6)a.

61 G.S. 160A-443(3)a. Service of orders is described in "Service of Complaints and Orders," above.

62. G.S. 160A-443(3)a. The "significant threat of bodily harm" calculus accounts not only for the current condition of the property, but also the nature of the repairs required and additional risks due to the presence of minors or disabled occupants. *Id.*

63. G.S. 160A-443(8). This particular provision actually requires the notice be sent upon a determination pursuant to subdivision (3) that a dwelling must be vacated and closed. Following the 2009 amendments, however, subdivision (3) no longer addresses vacate and close determinations, except for temporary vacate and close orders effective during the time allotted for repairs. A reasonable interpretation following the 2009 amendments is that the notification requirement becomes effective both upon issuance of a temporary vacate and close order pursuant to subdivision (3) and upon issuance of a long-term vacate and close order pursuant to subdivision (4).

64. G.S. 160A-443(4).

65. See note 54 above.

66. G.S. 160A-443(4). The language in the statute states that the governing body must order the public officer "to proceed to effectuate the purpose of this Article." *Id.* If this precise language is used in the ordinance adopted by the governing body, the ordinance could be interpreted as empowering the public officer to exercise his or her discretion in deciding whether to effectuate repair or to vacate and close a particular dwelling. It

is doubtful the statute's drafters intended for the public officer to make this decision on behalf of the board. Thus the governing board should specify in its ordinance which form of effectuation—repair or vacate and close—the public officer should undertake.

67. See note 55 above.

68. G.S. 160A-443(4).

69. G.S. 160A-443(6)a. This lien is described in Section 3.2.

70. See the discussion in note 63 above. The notification advised here remains consistent with the intent of the statute as it existed prior to 2009.

71. G.S. 160A-443(6)a.

72. *Id.* Minor variations in the wording of a posted notice are not material. Dale v. City of Morganton, 270 N.C. 567, 576, 155 S.E.2d 136, 144 (1967) (holding that the variation between the notice prescribed by the statute and the wording of a posted notice reading "THIS BUILDING IS UNSAFE, AND ITS USE FOR OCCUPANCY HAS BEEN PROHIBITED BY THE BUILDING OFFICIAL," was not material).

73. G.S. 160A-443(7). The procedural requirements of the civil action are described in detail in G.S. 160A-443(7) to include cross-references to the appropriate sections of the North Carolina General Statutes pertaining to summary ejectment: G.S. 42-29 (service of the summons and complaint), G.S. 42-30 (entering of the summary ejectment judgment), G.S. 7A-228 (appeal from any judgment entered by the magistrate), G.S. 7A-227 (stay of execution of magistrate's judgment).

74. Prior to the 2009 amendments, this particular option (effectuating repair of a dwelling after it has been vacated and closed) was not permissible. Under the original statutory scheme, the owner—not the local government—could decide whether to repair or to vacate and close a dwelling. When an owner chose the latter, it had basically fully complied with the local government order. To nullify the owner's compliance by repairing the dwelling—after the owner had elected to vacate and close it—seemed a violation of the owner's protections under the statute. Now, following the 2009 amendments, an owner is ordered simply to repair a dwelling and is offered no vacate and close opportunity. If the owner fails to comply, the local government—not the owner—elects whether to repair the dwelling or close it. Thus a reasonable interpretation of the statute could be that a local government may initially vacate and close a dwelling and later consider repairing it. Repair at some later point would require enactment of an ordinance—following a public hearing properly held in accordance with G.S. 160A-364 or G.S. 153A-323—directing the public officer to effectuate repair. But if prior to repair the dwelling's condition deteriorates to the point that it qualifies for demolition under the statute, then the local government loses its authority to repair the dwelling under subsection (4) of G.S. 160A-443. At that point, pursuant to subsection (5), a local government possesses authority only to remove or demolish the dwelling, and then only after the government restarts the order, notice, and hearing process. See note 46 above and accompanying text.

75. See note 46 above and accompanying text.

76. G.S. 160A-443(5a) and (5b).

77. S.L. 2009-279, sec. 7, G.S. 160A-443(3) through (8).

78. Prior to October 1, 2009, when the amendments enacted by S.L. 2009-279 became effective, local governments were not permitted to order an owner solely to repair a dwelling. Rather, the order gave owners a choice either "to repair . . . the dwelling in order to render it fit for human habitation or to vacate and close the dwelling . . . ." For a blackline comparison of the minimum housing statutes as they existed prior to 2009 with the statutes as modified by the 2009 amendments, see the version of S.L. 2009-279 posted on the North Carolina General Assembly website at www.ncga.state.nc.us/Sessions/2009/Bills/Senate/PDF/S661v6.pdf.

79. G.S. 160A-443(5a)a.

80. G.S. 160A-443(5a)b.

81. G.S. 160A-443(5b) (granting the same power as G.S. 160A-443(5a) and noting that "[t]his subdivision applies to the Cities of Eden, Lumberton, Roanoke Rapids, and Whiteville, to the municipalities in Lee County, and the Towns of Bethel, Farmville, Newport, and Waynesville only.").

82. The governing body must find that *all* of the following conditions exist: the dwelling would continue to deteriorate, it would create a fire and safety hazard, it would be a threat to children and vagrants, it would attract persons intent on criminal activities, it would cause or contribute to blight and the deterioration of property values in the area, and it would render unavailable property and a dwelling which might otherwise have been made available to ease the persistent shortage of decent and affordable housing in the state. G.S. 160A-443(5a) and (5b).

83. Enactment of an ordinance must be preceded by a public hearing properly held in accordance with G.S. 160A-364 or G.S. 153A-323. The ordinance must be served on the owner. This is the only instance where an ordinance—rather than an order—must be served on the owner. Personal service is required because the alternatives offered in G.S. 160A-445 apply to service of complaints or orders, not ordinances.

84. G.S. 160A-443(5a) (emphasis added). *See also* G.S. 160A-443(5b) (authorizing enumerated smaller municipalities to employ identical procedures).

85. G.S. 160A-443(5a) and (5b).

86. G.S. 160A-443(6)a. If the property is removed or demolished, the public officer must sell the materials and personal property in compliance with G.S. 160A-443(6)c.

87. G.S. 160A-443(3)a. Dwellings may be temporarily vacated and closed "during the time allowed for repair" if a threat of bodily harm or additional risks to occupants exist. *Id.* See also note 62 and accompanying text.

88. G.S. 160A-443(4).

89. Subdivisions (5a) and (5b) of G.S. 160A-443 indicate that abandonment of intent to repair procedures become operative either one year following adoption of a permanent vacate and close ordinance pursuant to subsection (4) or one year following adoption of a temporary vacate and close order pursuant to subsection (3)a.

90. See notes 74–76 above and accompanying text.

91. G.S. 160A-443(5a) and (5b).

92. Repair activity must be purposeful and meaningful after one year. Otherwise, a governing board can still determine that an owner has abandoned the intent and purpose to repair, and, if eligible, use that determination as the basis for proceeding under the abandonment of intent to repair procedures.

93. Due process considerations may include any changes over time in the status of a dwelling, changes in ownership of a dwelling, and excessive periods of delay between the expiration of the time allowed for repair and the time at which a local government seeks to effectuate a repair order. No North Carolina case law sheds light on the limits of local government delay.

94. If the dwelling has deteriorated to the point it is eligible for demolition, the local government may no longer repair it under subsection (4) of G.S. 160A-443. Authority for a local government to effectuate a repair order exists only while the cost of repairing the dwelling is below the threshold set in the minimum housing ordinance. Once that cost threshold is exceeded, the local government is authorized only to remove or demolish pursuant to subsection (5) and only after it restarts the process to obtain a demolition order. Restarting the process requires new notice and a new hearing prior to demolition. See note 46 above and accompanying text.

95. If some indication exists that the owners have begun making repairs within the time period allotted in the order to repair, the public officer is prohibited from effectuating the

order until the time allotted for repair elapses. *See* Wiggins v. City of Monroe, 73 N.C. App. 44, 48, 326 S.E.2d 39, 42 (1985) (holding that once the owners began making repairs within the time limit set by the public officer, the officer had no authority to pursue effectuation until the allotted repair period had elapsed).

96. G.S. 160A-446(a).

97. G.S. 160A-446(b).

98. G.S. 160A-446(a).

99. *See* Harrell v. City of Winston-Salem, 22 N.C. App. 386, 391–92, 206 S.E.2d 802, 806 (1974) (affirming summary judgment for defendant city because "plaintiffs must exhaust the administrative remedies available to them, and they cannot be allowed to undermine the prescribed statutory procedure set forth in G.S. 160A-446."); Axler v. City of Wilmington, 25 N.C. App. 110, 112, 212 S.E.2d 510, 511 (1975) ("Plaintiff failed to utilize the administrative remedies available to him and failed to follow the statutory procedures set out in G.S. 160A-446. For these reasons it was proper to dismiss this action against the city.").

100. G.S. 160A-446(d).

101. G.S. 160A-388(a); G.S. 153A-345(a).

102. G.S. 160A-388(e); G.S. 153A-345(e).

103. G.S. 160A-446(d). When hearing appeals, the appeals board sits as a quasi-judicial body. For analysis of quasi-judicial bodies in a related context, see *Coffey v. Town of Waynesville,* 143 N.C. App. 624, 629, 547 S.E.2d 132, 135 (2001). *See also* Owens, note 15 above, at 107–19.

104. G.S. 160A-446(c).

105. *Id.*

106. *Id.*

107. *Id.*

108. *Id.*

109. G.S. 160A-446(e). This fifteen-day requirement for minimum housing appeals is shorter than the thirty-day requirement applicable to most decisions of zoning boards of adjustment under G.S. 160A-388(e2). This inconsistency is not resolved by other statutes or case law. However, the shorter fifteen-day period, which is specifically assigned for petitions related to minimum housing decisions, probably trumps the more general thirty-day period allowed for appeal from other decisions by a zoning board of adjustment. The shorter period for minimum housing appeals can be explained, however, because such appeals, which involve "dangerous or injurious" conditions, necessarily demand greater urgency than typical zoning cases. *Cf.* G.S. 160A-446(f) (demonstrating a similar sense of urgency for minimum housing hearings held in superior court, which "shall be given preference over other matters on the court's calendar").

110. G.S. 160A-446(f).

111. *Id.*

112. G.S. 160A-449.

113. *Id.* An example of earmarked revenues would be enterprise fund revenues collected for a public utility.

114. G.S. 160A-443(6)a. ("[T]he amount of the cost of repairs, alterations or improvements, or vacating and closing, or removal or demolition by the public officer shall be a lien against the real property upon which the cost was incurred, which lien shall be filed, have the same priority, and be collected as the lien for special assessment provided in Article 10 of this Chapter.").

115. Special assessment liens are identical to property tax liens except they are by statute junior to any local, state, or federal tax liens. G.S. 160A-233(c) (cities) and G.S. 153A-200 (counties).

116. Special assessments may be collected "in the same manner as property taxes," meaning local governments may use garnishment and attachment of personal property (including bank accounts, wages, and other assets) in addition to real property foreclosure remedies. G.S. 160A-228 (cities) and G.S. 153A-195 (counties).

117. *See, e.g.,* G.S. 105-362; G.S. 105-375(i).

118. G.S. 160A-443(6)b.

119. *Id.*

120. Homebuilders Ass'n. of Charlotte, Inc. v. City of Charlotte, 336 N.C. 37, 46, 442 S.E.2d 45, 51 (1994). See also the discussion of fees in Section 2.4.

121. *See* Newton v. City of Winston-Salem, 92 N.C. App. 446, 449, 374 S.E.2d 488, 491 (1988) ("The statute specifically states that cities and counties may exercise such powers *only* 'in the manner herein provided.'") (emphasis added, citation omitted). See also Chapter 2, notes 71–72 and accompanying text.

122. *See* G.S. 160A-449.

123. G.S. 160A-443(6). Fees are permitted to be levied on residential rental property provided the fee is also levied on other commercial and residential property. Otherwise, fees may be levied on residential rental property only when it is identified as a problem property. See Chapter 2, note 63.

124. Fines and civil penalties may be imposed for the unlawful occupation of a dwelling on which a placard has been posted pursuant to G.S. 160A-443(4).

125. G.S. 160A-175 (cities) and G.S. 153A-123 (counties).

126. See note 121 above.

127. See Chapter 2, note 69 and accompanying text.

128. G.S. 153A-123(g) and G.S. 160A-174(g). A secondary argument may provide additional support for this conclusion. The intent of the legislature in enacting the minimum housing statutes could not have included a grant of authority for fines and penalties. When the minimum housing statutes were first enacted, local governments did not enjoy any general authority to enforce ordinances. At that time, Dillon's Rule restricted local government authority only to that specifically granted by statute, so a failure to include authority to assess fines or penalties effectively amounted to a prohibition. Therefore, an argument can be made that the legislature never intended to permit local governments to use fines or penalties to enforce minimum housing standards. Alternatively—illustrating the difficulty in making conclusions about legislative intent—in the time since the legislature enacted the general authority to enforce local ordinances, it has not acted to specifically prohibit fines or penalties in the minimum housing context.

129. See notes 50–51 above and accompanying text.

130. Press Release, U.S. Census Bureau, Florida, California and Texas to Dominate Future Population Growth (Apr. 21, 2005), www.census.gov/newsroom/releases/archives/population/cb05-52.html.

131. See G.S. 160A-444 ("The ordinances [adopted by a city under this Part] may provide additional standards to guide the public officers, or his agents, in determining the fitness of a dwelling for human habitation.").

132. See Section 2.5.

133. While this list is hypothetical, all of the listed conditions are taken from existing minimum housing ordinances in North Carolina.

134. See Section 3.1 (discussing preliminary investigation, notice, and service requirements).

135. G.S. 160A-443(6)a.

136. *See* G.S. 160A-175(a) and (c) (cities) and G.S. 153A-123(a) and (c) (counties).

# 4

# The Design of Comprehensive Repair-Oriented Housing Codes: Applying the General Police Power and Minimum Housing Authority Together

Using the information presented thus far, it would be fairly straightforward to design an ordinance regulating the outward appearance of dwellings, to include aesthetic features such as ornamental light fixtures, a decorative fence, or an accessory building not used for human habitation. To regulate such features, an ordinance could be enacted under the general police power following the guidelines presented in Chapter 2. As discussed there, some local governments find it necessary to regulate the outward appearance of dwellings at an early stage in order to preserve property values, reduce crime, and prevent the spread of blight. The minimum housing statutes would not be relevant or applicable—aesthetic features of dwellings do not pertain to fitness for human habitation and therefore are not regulated pursuant to the minimum housing statutes.

However, a minimum housing ordinance is the only means of regulating substandard components of a dwelling that pertain to a dwelling's fitness for human habitation. Case law dictates that these components may be regulated only in the manner provided by the minimum housing statutes.[1] Chapter 3 examined how minimum housing ordinances operate.

Rarely, however, will a deteriorating dwelling fit neatly into only one category. Typically, such a dwelling will be substandard in both its outward appearance and its fitness for human habitation. A comprehensive repair-oriented regulation would address both types of substandard conditions. Given the separate spheres to which the general police power and the minimum housing statutes apply in this context, a comprehensive approach presents some challenges. To illustrate these challenges, a hypothetical comprehensive repair-oriented housing code will be examined in light of how it might function when applied to a dwelling that exhibits both types of substandard conditions: some that render the dwelling unfit for human habitation, and others that pertain only to the dwelling's outward appearance.

A comprehensive housing code would likely contain the following major components: (1) enumeration of standards of maintenance in terms of both outward appearance and fitness for human habitation, (2) procedures for effectuation by the local government in case of owner noncompliance with orders issued pursuant to the code, (3) cost recoupment following effectuation, (4) fines or penalties, and (5) fees to cover administration. Each component will be examined below in terms of how it would need to be designed in order to account for the two different sets of authority under which deteriorating dwellings may be regulated.

## 4.1 Enumeration of Standards of Maintenance

The centerpiece of a comprehensive repair-oriented housing code would be the standards of maintenance applicable to deteriorating dwellings. These standards would enumerate the various substandard conditions, such as a broken light fixture or a hole in the roof, that would be considered violations of the comprehensive housing code.

Issuing such standards in a single aggregated form without reference to the two primary sources of authority for regulating dwellings might be possible, but doing so may lead to confusion when code enforcement is attempted. Such confusion arises because enforcement mechanisms and procedures differ according to which source of authority—minimum housing or general police power—applies to a particular standard.

Thus, creating two sets of standards may be helpful in formulating a comprehensive housing code. The first set of standards would pertain to a dwelling's fitness for human habitation. Aspects of a dwelling that fail to meet those standards would be regulated pursuant to the minimum housing statutes. The second set of standards would pertain to a dwelling's outward appearance. It would set standards for features that have no bearing on a dwelling's fitness for human habitation but must be kept in good repair nonetheless. Aspects of a dwelling that violate these good repair standards would be regulated pursuant to the general police power.

As will be discussed below in the examination of other parts of the comprehensive code, bifurcating the standards pays dividends later. It clarifies statutory authority and makes it easier to delineate two sets of procedures for activities such as local government effectuation, cost recoupment, collection of administrative fees, and imposition of penalties.

## 4.2 Procedures for Local Government Effectuation in the Event of Owner Noncompliance

Consider a dwelling that is in a state of disrepair. Some of the dwelling's substandard components pertain to its fitness (such as a hole in the roof), and the rest of the substandard components pertain to its outward appearance (such as a broken exterior light fixture over the front door). The public officer notifies the owner about the substandard conditions, but the owner takes no action to make repairs. A comprehensive code must contain detailed procedures for handling the owner's noncompliance and for effectuating repairs if necessary.

Having two sources of regulatory authority in North Carolina with two different sets of procedures for effectuation complicates enforcement of comprehensive housing codes. The public officer cannot use a single set of procedures to address all of the code violations because there are actually two distinct sets of procedures. Which set should be used depends on the standard being enforced. For enforcement of standards pertaining to a dwelling's fitness for human habitation, minimum housing procedures must be employed, and these consist of administrative—rather than judicial—proceedings all the way through effectuation.[2] It is only upon appeal—and then only after the appeals board renders a decision (if an appeals board has been established)—that an owner can go to court.

Contrast these procedures with those related to the enforcement of good-repair standards governing a dwelling's outward appearance—that is, standards applicable to components with no bearing on fitness but which nonetheless must be maintained in good repair. Court involvement is necessary almost from the start. Local government effectuation is permitted exclusively by authority of a court-issued contempt citation which is issued only after the owner fails to comply with an earlier court order.[3]

A public officer could proceed by enforcing only one set of standards or both, but if enforcing both, the officer must employ two different sets of procedures and each must be initiated independently of the other. For this reason, the separate enforcement procedures required by the two different sources of authority—the minimum housing statutes and the general police power—should remain bifurcated in a comprehensive code. The need for such bifurcation clarifies why the maintenance standards discussed in Section 4.1 should be bifurcated as well. The division of standards into two categories will aid the public officer in enforcing the standards—and perhaps effectuating repairs—under the two completely different sets of procedures.


## 4.3 Cost Recoupment for Effectuation

Say that the dwelling in our example is not repaired by the owner and the public officer successfully effectuates repair of all the substandard conditions (using minimum housing procedures for the repairs pertaining to fitness and using contempt citations for the rest). The public officer may then take steps to recoup the costs incurred by effectuation, but the recoupment mechanisms are different depending on the conditions repaired. For repairs effectuated using minimum housing procedures, the costs of effectuation become a high-priority lien on the property. This lien is collected as a lien for a special assessment, which is collected in the same way as a property tax lien.[4] These liens survive foreclosure and can be pursued using robust collection methods.[5] For the other repairs—effectuated in reliance on the general police power—the costs of effectuation become a relatively low-priority mechanics lien on the owner's property.[6]

As a result of effectuating repairs pursuant to a comprehensive housing code, the public officer may have to levy two separate liens on the property: one for costs incurred pursuant to the minimum housing statutes and another lien of lower priority for the remaining costs. To ensure this bifurcated recoupment authority is administered properly, the two recoupment methods should remain separated and clearly aligned with the appropriate set of standards to which they apply—either the set that pertains to the dwelling's fitness for human habitation or the set that does not.


## 4.4 Fines and Penalties

Some local governments may consider adding a punitive component to a comprehensive housing code. Given the revenue-generating advantage penalties hold over fines, civil penalties—rather than fines—likely will be included in most codes.[7] One can imagine penalties for violating maintenance standards or for failing to comply with orders in a timely manner.

Whatever penalties are devised, local governments must be clear about which set of standards is the source of the penalty. Civil penalties cannot be used to enforce regulations related to a dwelling's fitness for human habitation;[8] they can be assessed only for violations of standards being enforced through the general police power.[9]

Once again, the value of maintaining two sets of standards is apparent. If the two sets of standards were collapsed into one without differentiating between those that pertain to a dwelling's fitness for human habitation and those that do not, a public officer might unintentionally assess a penalty without the legal authority to do so.

## 4.5 Fees to Cover Administrative Costs

In enforcing a comprehensive housing code, the public officer will perform inspections, issue notices, hold hearings, and engage in enforcement-related activities. A comprehensive code could include a schedule of fees to be paid by owners whose poorly maintained property enters the enforcement process and requires attention from the public officer. Unlike other parts of a comprehensive code, the authority for charging fees is the same regardless of the condition being regulated; it is the only part of the code that does not require separate treatment for each of the sources of authority. Thus, a local government can develop a single schedule of fees to be applied regardless of whether the conditions being regulated pertain to a dwelling's fitness.[10] Recall, however, that authority to charge fees is limited under case law to a reasonable amount designed only to offset the costs of the regulatory activity.

## 4.6 Alternatives to Strict Bifurcation

A common thread runs through the above examination of a comprehensive repair-oriented housing code: local governments must pay close attention to differences between actions taken pursuant to the general police power and those taken pursuant to minimum housing statutes. This concern will persist until state law overrules *Newton* by specifically permitting local governments to use their general police power—and not solely the minimum housing statutes—to regulate unfit dwellings.[11] If statewide legislation were enacted to overrule *Newton*, local governments would not have to worry about the dividing line between the general police power and minimum housing statutes. Rather, in situations in which public officials were unsure which authority applied, they could move forward with confidence under the general police power. In the absence of statewide legislation, a local government could pursue a local act to achieve this result in its jurisdiction. Even without such legislative action, however, local governments possess ample authority to enact comprehensive repair-oriented housing codes, provided they carefully navigate the procedural complexities and observe the legal limitations described in this publication.

## Notes

1. See Chapter 2, notes 71–77 and accompanying text.
2. See Section 3.1.
3. See Section 2.3.
4. See Section 3.2.
5. *Id.*
6. See Section 2.3.
7. See Section 2.4.
8. See Section 3.2 (discussing the impermissibility of assessing fees to enforce minimum housing ordinances).
9. See Section 2.4 (discussing civil penalties for violations of ordinances enacted pursuant to the general police power).
10. See Section 2.4 (discussing fees under the general police power) and Section 3.2 (discussing fees under the minimum housing statutes). Recall that fees designed to single out residential rental properties are prohibited except under certain conditions set forth by statute. See Chapter 2, note 63; Chapter 3, note 123.
11. For a more detailed discussion of this possibility and an exploration of other policy options, see C. Tyler Mulligan, *Toward a Comprehensive Program for Regulating Vacant or Abandoned Dwellings in North Carolina: The General Police Power, Minimum Housing Standards, and Vacant Property Registration*, 32 CAMPBELL L. REV. 1, 46–49 (2009).

# Appendix 1
## Minimum Housing Procedures Flowchart

## A. The Determination of Unfitness

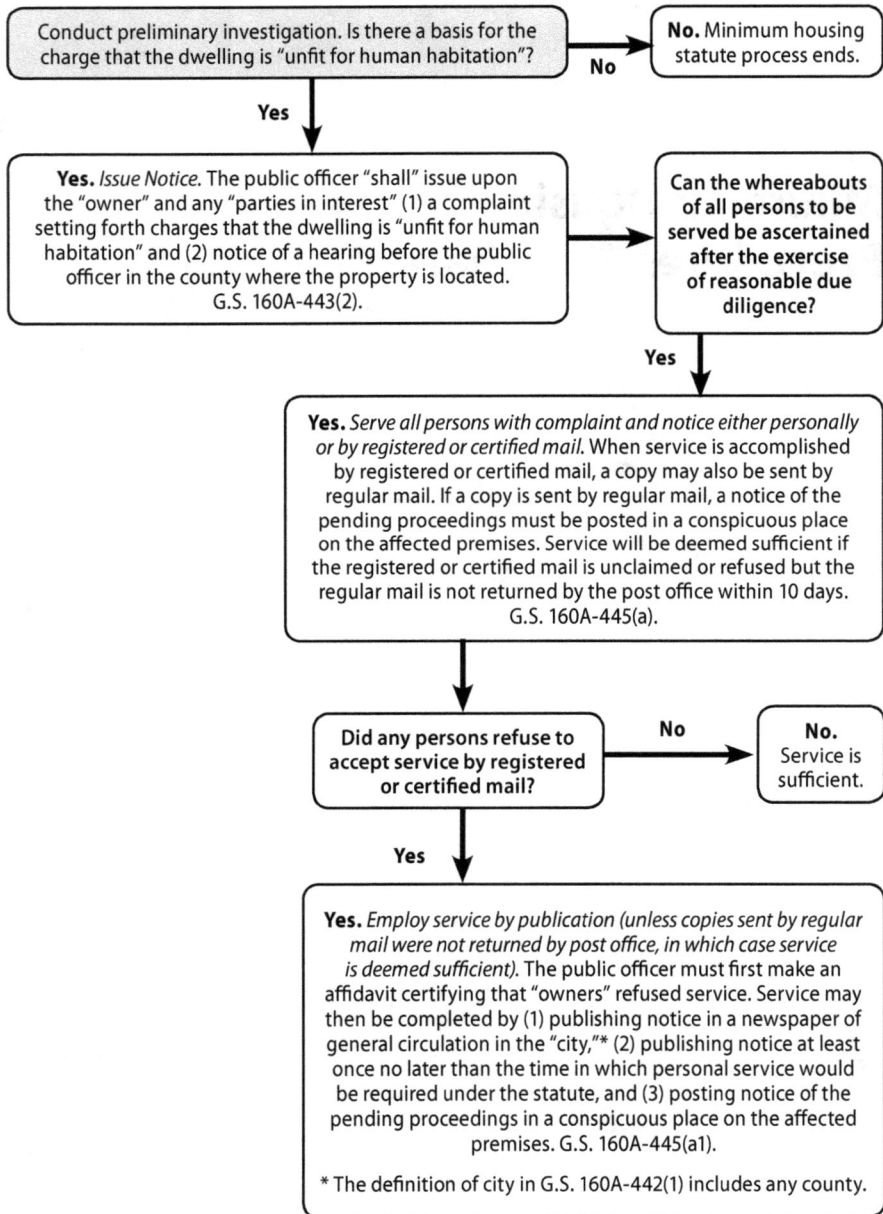

Conduct preliminary investigation. Is there a basis for the charge that the dwelling is "unfit for human habitation"?

**No** → **No.** Minimum housing statute process ends.

**Yes** ↓

**Yes.** *Issue Notice.* The public officer "shall" issue upon the "owner" and any "parties in interest" (1) a complaint setting forth charges that the dwelling is "unfit for human habitation" and (2) notice of a hearing before the public officer in the county where the property is located. G.S. 160A-443(2).

→ Can the whereabouts of all persons to be served be ascertained after the exercise of reasonable due diligence?

**No** →

**Yes** ↓

**Yes.** *Serve all persons with complaint and notice either personally or by registered or certified mail.* When service is accomplished by registered or certified mail, a copy may also be sent by regular mail. If a copy is sent by regular mail, a notice of the pending proceedings must be posted in a conspicuous place on the affected premises. Service will be deemed sufficient if the registered or certified mail is unclaimed or refused but the regular mail is not returned by the post office within 10 days. G.S. 160A-445(a).

↓

Did any persons refuse to accept service by registered or certified mail?

**No** → **No.** Service is sufficient.

**Yes** ↓

**Yes.** *Employ service by publication (unless copies sent by regular mail were not returned by post office, in which case service is deemed sufficient).* The public officer must first make an affidavit certifying that "owners" refused service. Service may then be completed by (1) publishing notice in a newspaper of general circulation in the "city,"* (2) publishing notice at least once no later than the time in which personal service would be required under the statute, and (3) posting notice of the pending proceedings in a conspicuous place on the affected premises. G.S. 160A-445(a1).

* The definition of city in G.S. 160A-442(1) includes any county.

**No.** *Employ service by publication.* The public officer must first make an affidavit certifying that the identities of owners or whereabouts of persons are unknown and cannot be ascertained in the exercise of reasonable diligence. Service may then be completed by (1) publishing notice in a newspaper of general circulation in the "city,"* (2) publishing notice at least once no later than the time in which personal service would be required under the statute, and (3) posting notice of the pending proceedings in a conspicuous place on the affected premises. G.S. 160A-445(a1).

* The definition of city in G.S. 160A-442(1) includes any county.

---

*Hold hearing.* The hearing on whether a dwelling is "unfit for human habitation" must take place not less than 10 days and not more than 30 days after publication or service of the complaint. G.S. 160A-443(2).

Does public officer determine that dwelling is "unfit for human habitation"?

**No** → **No.** Minimum housing statute process ends.

**Yes**

**Yes.** *Go to "B. Initial Minimum Housing Ordinance Orders."*

## B. Initial Minimum Housing Ordinance Orders Subsequent to the Determination of Unfitness

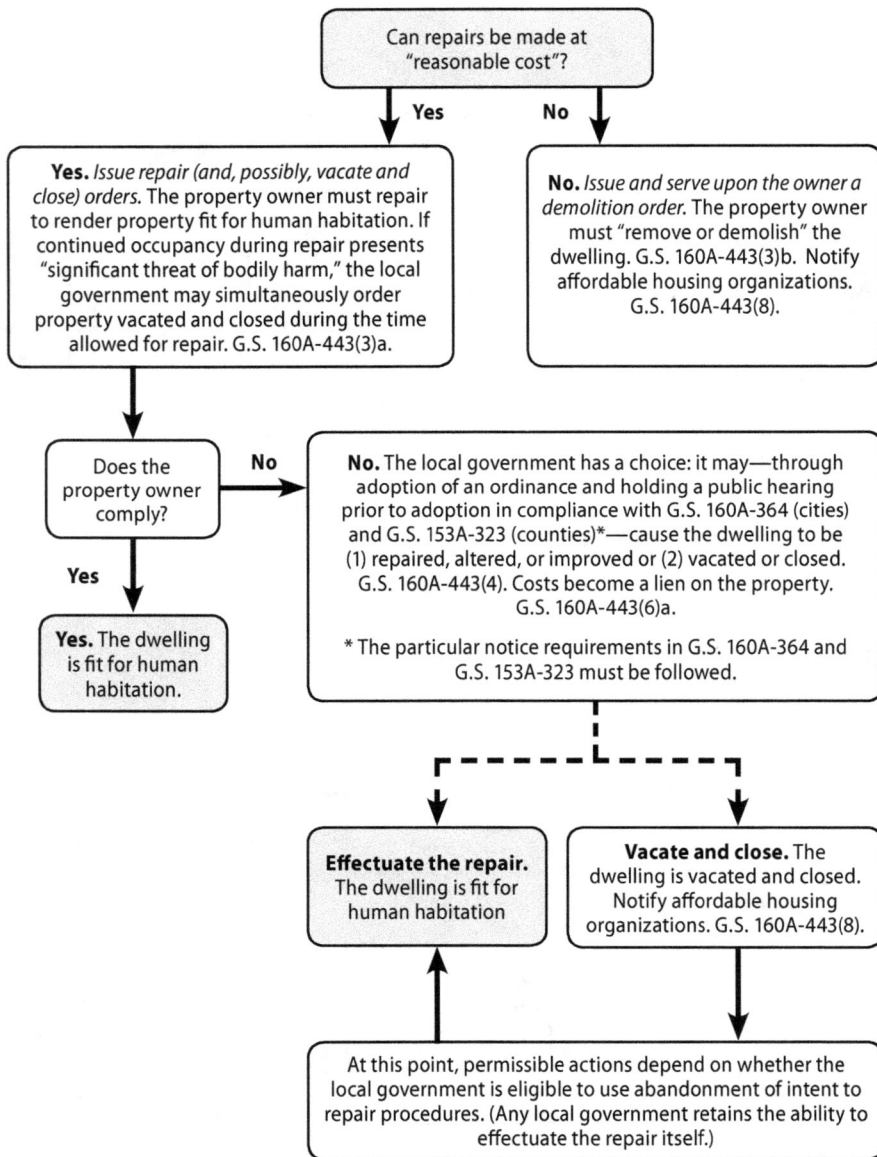

Can repairs be made at "reasonable cost"?

Yes      No

**Yes.** *Issue repair (and, possibly, vacate and close) orders.* The property owner must repair to render property fit for human habitation. If continued occupancy during repair presents "significant threat of bodily harm," the local government may simultaneously order property vacated and closed during the time allowed for repair. G.S. 160A-443(3)a.

**No.** *Issue and serve upon the owner a demolition order.* The property owner must "remove or demolish" the dwelling. G.S. 160A-443(3)b. Notify affordable housing organizations. G.S. 160A-443(8).

Does the property owner comply?

**No**

Yes

**Yes.** The dwelling is fit for human habitation.

**No.** The local government has a choice: it may—through adoption of an ordinance and holding a public hearing prior to adoption in compliance with G.S. 160A-364 (cities) and G.S. 153A-323 (counties)*—cause the dwelling to be (1) repaired, altered, or improved or (2) vacated or closed. G.S. 160A-443(4). Costs become a lien on the property. G.S. 160A-443(6)a.

\* The particular notice requirements in G.S. 160A-364 and G.S. 153A-323 must be followed.

**Effectuate the repair.** The dwelling is fit for human habitation

**Vacate and close.** The dwelling is vacated and closed. Notify affordable housing organizations. G.S. 160A-443(8).

At this point, permissible actions depend on whether the local government is eligible to use abandonment of intent to repair procedures. (Any local government retains the ability to effectuate the repair itself.)

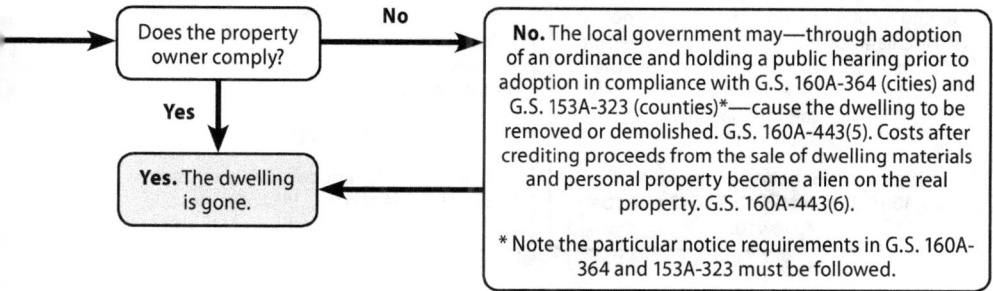

Does the property owner comply?

**No** →

**No.** The local government may—through adoption of an ordinance and holding a public hearing prior to adoption in compliance with G.S. 160A-364 (cities) and G.S. 153A-323 (counties)*—cause the dwelling to be removed or demolished. G.S. 160A-443(5). Costs after crediting proceeds from the sale of dwelling materials and personal property become a lien on the real property. G.S. 160A-443(6).

* Note the particular notice requirements in G.S. 160A-364 and 153A-323 must be followed.

**Yes**

**Yes.** The dwelling is gone.

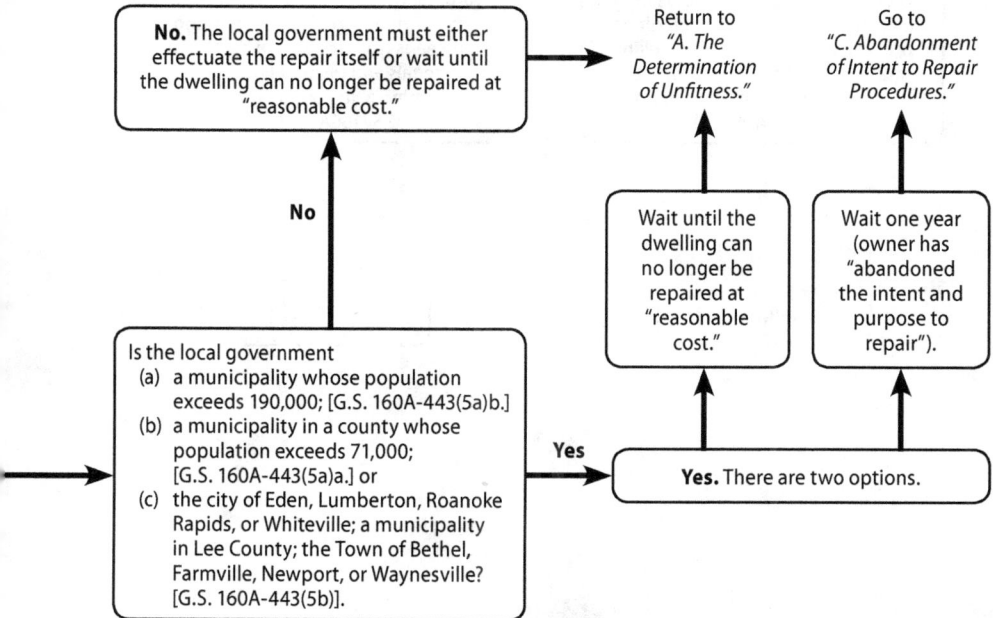

**No.** The local government must either effectuate the repair itself or wait until the dwelling can no longer be repaired at "reasonable cost."

Return to *"A. The Determination of Unfitness."*

Go to *"C. Abandonment of Intent to Repair Procedures."*

**No**

Wait until the dwelling can no longer be repaired at "reasonable cost."

Wait one year (owner has "abandoned the intent and purpose to repair").

Is the local government
(a) a municipality whose population exceeds 190,000; [G.S. 160A-443(5a)b.]
(b) a municipality in a county whose population exceeds 71,000; [G.S. 160A-443(5a)a.] or
(c) the city of Eden, Lumberton, Roanoke Rapids, or Whiteville; a municipality in Lee County; the Town of Bethel, Farmville, Newport, or Waynesville? [G.S. 160A-443(5b)].

**Yes** →

**Yes.** There are two options.

# C. Abandonment of Intent to Repair Procedures

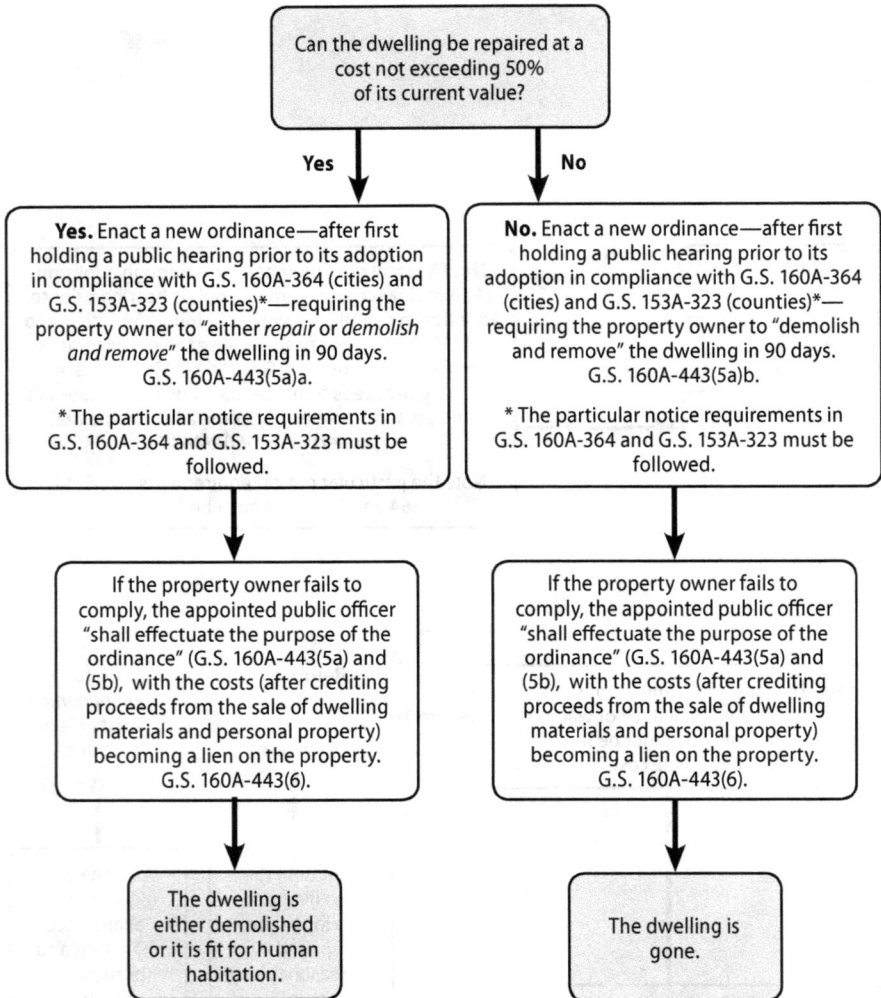

Can the dwelling be repaired at a cost not exceeding 50% of its current value?

**Yes**

**No**

**Yes.** Enact a new ordinance—after first holding a public hearing prior to its adoption in compliance with G.S. 160A-364 (cities) and G.S. 153A-323 (counties)*—requiring the property owner to "either *repair* or *demolish and remove*" the dwelling in 90 days. G.S. 160A-443(5a)a.

\* The particular notice requirements in G.S. 160A-364 and G.S. 153A-323 must be followed.

**No.** Enact a new ordinance—after first holding a public hearing prior to its adoption in compliance with G.S. 160A-364 (cities) and G.S. 153A-323 (counties)*—requiring the property owner to "demolish and remove" the dwelling in 90 days. G.S. 160A-443(5a)b.

\* The particular notice requirements in G.S. 160A-364 and G.S. 153A-323 must be followed.

If the property owner fails to comply, the appointed public officer "shall effectuate the purpose of the ordinance" (G.S. 160A-443(5a) and (5b), with the costs (after crediting proceeds from the sale of dwelling materials and personal property) becoming a lien on the property. G.S. 160A-443(6).

If the property owner fails to comply, the appointed public officer "shall effectuate the purpose of the ordinance" (G.S. 160A-443(5a) and (5b), with the costs (after crediting proceeds from the sale of dwelling materials and personal property) becoming a lien on the property. G.S. 160A-443(6).

The dwelling is either demolished or it is fit for human habitation.

The dwelling is gone.

Appendix 2
# Affidavit to Obtain Administrative Inspection Warrant

(TYPE OR PRINT IN BLACK INK)

## STATE OF NORTH CAROLINA
In The General Court Of Justice

_____ County

**AFFIDAVIT TO OBTAIN
ADMINISTRATIVE INSPECTION
WARRANT FOR PARTICULAR
CONDITION OR ACTIVITY**

I, _____ , being
_(name and position)_

duly sworn and examined under oath, state under oath that there is probable cause for believing that there is

_____
_(describe condition, object, activity, or circumstance which the search is intended to check or reveal)_
_____
_____

at the property owned or possessed by _____

and described as follows: _____

_____
_(precisely describe the property to be inspected)_

The facts which establish probable cause to believe this are: _____

_____
_____
_____
_____
_____
_____
_____

Signature Of Applicant

Name Of Applicant (Type Or Print)

### SWORN AND SUBSCRIBED TO BEFORE ME:

Date

Signature

| | | |
|---|---|---|
| ☐ Deputy CSC | ☐ Assistant CSC | ☐ Clerk Of Superior Court |
| ☐ Magistrate | ☐ District Court Judge | ☐ Superior Court Judge |

**IMPORTANT:** _Attach the Affidavit to the WARRANT if not on reverse side._

*(TYPE OR PRINT IN BLACK INK)*

| | |
|---|---|
| **STATE OF NORTH CAROLINA**<br>In The General Court Of Justice<br>_____ County | **ADMINISTRATIVE INSPECTION**<br>**WARRANT FOR PARTICULAR**<br>**CONDITION OR ACTIVITY**<br>G.S. 15-27.2; 58-79-1 |

**TO ANY LAWFUL OFFICIAL EMPOWERED TO CONDUCT THE INSPECTION AUTHORIZED BY THIS WARRANT:**

The applicant named on the accompanying affidavit, which is hereby incorporated by reference, being duly sworn, has stated to me that there is a condition, object, activity, or circumstance legally justifying an inspection of the property described in that affidavit. I have examined this applicant under oath or affirmation and have verified the accuracy of the matters in the affidavit establishing the legal grounds for this Warrant. YOU ARE HEREBY COMMANDED TO INSPECT THE PROPERTY DESCRIBED IN THE ACCOMPANYING AFFIDAVIT.

This inspection is authorized to check or reveal the conditions, objects, activities, or circumstances indicated in the accompanying affidavit.

This Warrant must be served upon the owner or possessor of the property described in the accompanying affidavit. If the owner or possessor is not present on the property at the time of inspection and you have made reasonable but unsuccessful efforts to locate the owner or possessor, you may instead serve it by affixing this Warrant or a copy to the property.

THIS WARRANT MAY BE EXECUTED ONLY BETWEEN THE HOURS OF 8:00 A.M. AND 8:00 P.M. AND ONLY WITHIN 24 HOURS AFTER IT WAS ISSUED. IT MUST BE RETURNED WITHIN 48 HOURS AFTER IT WAS ISSUED. HOWEVER, IF THIS WARRANT IS ISSUED PURSUANT TO A FIRE INVESTIGATION AUTHORIZED BY G.S. 58-79-1, IT MAY BE EXECUTED AT ANY TIME WITHIN 48 HOURS AFTER IT IS ISSUED. IT MUST BE RETURNED WITHOUT UNNECESSARY DELAY AFTER ITS EXECUTION OR AFTER 48 HOURS FROM THE TIME IT WAS ISSUED IF IT WAS NOT EXECUTED.

| Date | Time | ☐ AM   ☐ PM |
|---|---|---|
| Signature | | |

☐ Deputy CSC ☐ Assistant CSC ☐ Clerk Of Superior Court
☐ Magistrate ☐ District Court Judge ☐ Superior Court Judge

### OFFICER'S RETURN

I certify that this WARRANT was executed on the date and time shown below.

| Date Of Execution | Signature Of Inspecting Official |
|---|---|
| Time Of Execution ☐ AM ☐ PM | Name Of Inspecting Official (Type Or Print) |

### CLERK'S ACCEPTANCE

This WARRANT has been returned to this office on the date and time shown below.

| Date Of Return | Signature |
|---|---|
| Time Of Return ☐ AM ☐ PM | ☐ Deputy CSC ☐ Assistant CSC ☐ Clerk Of Superior Court |

**IMPORTANT:** *Attach the Affidavit to the WARRANT if not on reverse side.*

AOC-CR-913M, Side Two, Rev. 7/01
© 2001 Administrative Office of the Courts

# Appendix 3
# Related Statutes

## General Police Power of Counties

### § 153A-4. Broad construction.

It is the policy of the General Assembly that the counties of this State should have adequate authority to exercise the powers, rights, duties, functions, privileges, and immunities conferred upon them by law. To this end, the provisions of this Chapter and of local acts shall be broadly construed and grants of power shall be construed to include any powers that are reasonably expedient to the exercise of the power.

### § 153A-121. General ordinance-making power.

(a)     A county may by ordinance define, regulate, prohibit, or abate acts, omissions, or conditions detrimental to the health, safety, or welfare of its citizens and the peace and dignity of the county; and may define and abate nuisances.

(b)     This section does not authorize a county to regulate or control vehicular or pedestrian traffic on a street or highway under the control of the Board of Transportation, nor to regulate or control any right-of-way or right-of-passage belonging to a public utility, electric or telephone membership corporation, or public agency of the State. In addition, no county ordinance may regulate or control a highway right-of-way in a manner inconsistent with State law or an ordinance of the Board of Transportation.

(c)     This section does not impair the authority of local boards of health to adopt rules and regulations to protect and promote public health.

### § 153A-123. Enforcement of ordinances.

(a)     A county may provide for fines and penalties for violation of its ordinances and may secure injunctions and abatement orders to further insure compliance with its ordinances, as provided by this section.

(b)     Unless the board of commissioners has provided otherwise, violation of a county ordinance is a misdemeanor or infraction as provided by G.S. 14-4. An ordinance may provide by express statement that the maximum fine, term of imprisonment, or infraction penalty to be imposed for a violation is some amount of money or number of days less than the maximum imposed by G.S. 14-4.

(c)     An ordinance may provide that violation subjects the offender to a civil penalty to be recovered by the county in a civil action in the nature of debt if the offender does not pay the penalty within a prescribed period of time after he has been cited for violation of the ordinance.

(c1)     An ordinance may provide for the recovery of a civil penalty by the county for violation of the fire prevention code of the State Building Code as authorized under G.S. 143-139.

(d)     An ordinance may provide that it may be enforced by an appropriate equitable remedy issuing from a court of competent jurisdiction. In such a case, the General Court of Justice has jurisdiction to issue any order that may be appropriate, and it is not a defense to the county's application for equitable relief that there is an adequate remedy at law.

(e)     An ordinance that makes unlawful a condition existing upon or use made of real property may provide that it may be enforced by injunction and order of abatement, and the General Court of Justice has jurisdiction to issue such an order. When a violation of such an ordinance occurs, the county may apply to the appropriate division of the General Court of Justice for a mandatory or prohibitory injunction and order of abatement commanding the defendant to correct the unlawful condition upon or cease the unlawful use of the property. The action shall be governed in all respects by the laws and rules governing civil proceedings, including the Rules of Civil Procedure in general and Rule 65 in particular.

In addition to an injunction, the court may enter an order of abatement as a part of the judgment in the cause. An order of abatement may direct that buildings or other structures on the property be closed, demolished, or removed; that fixtures, furniture, or other movable property be removed from buildings on the property; that grass and weeds be cut; that improvements or repairs be made; or that any other action be taken that is necessary to bring the property into compliance with the ordinance. If the defendant fails or refuses to comply with an injunction or with an order of abatement within the time allowed by the court, he may be cited for contempt and the county may execute the order of abatement. If the county executes the order, it has a lien on the property, in the nature of a mechanic's and materialman's lien, for the costs of executing the order. The defendant may secure cancellation of an order of abatement by paying all costs of the proceedings and posting a bond for compliance with the order. The bond shall be given with sureties approved by the clerk of superior court in an amount approved by the judge before whom the matter was heard and shall be conditioned on the defendant's full compliance with the terms of the order of abatement within the time fixed by the judge. Cancellation of an order of abatement does not suspend or cancel an injunction issued in conjunction with the order.

(f)    Subject to the express terms of the ordinance, a county ordinance may be enforced by any one or more of the remedies authorized by this section.

(g)    A county ordinance may provide, when appropriate, that each day's continuing violation is a separate and distinct offense.

## General Police Power of Cities

### § 160A-4. Broad construction.

It is the policy of the General Assembly that the cities of this State should have adequate authority to execute the powers, duties, privileges, and immunities conferred upon them by law. To this end, the provisions of this Chapter and of city charters shall be broadly construed and grants of power shall be construed to include any additional and supplementary powers that are reasonably necessary or expedient to carry them into execution and effect: Provided, that the exercise of such additional or supplementary powers shall not be contrary to State or federal law or to the public policy of this State.

### § 160A-174. General ordinance-making power.

(a)    A city may by ordinance define, prohibit, regulate, or abate acts, omissions, or conditions, detrimental to the health, safety, or welfare of its citizens and the peace and dignity of the city, and may define and abate nuisances.

(b)    A city ordinance shall be consistent with the Constitution and laws of North Carolina and of the United States. An ordinance is not consistent with State or federal law when:

> (1)    The ordinance infringes a liberty guaranteed to the people by the State or federal Constitution;
> (2)    The ordinance makes unlawful an act, omission or condition which is expressly made lawful by State or federal law;

(3)    The ordinance makes lawful an act, omission, or condition which is expressly made unlawful by State or federal law;

(4)    The ordinance purports to regulate a subject that cities are expressly forbidden to regulate by State or federal law;

(5)    The ordinance purports to regulate a field for which a State or federal statute clearly shows a legislative intent to provide a complete and integrated regulatory scheme to the exclusion of local regulation;

(6)    The elements of an offense defined by a city ordinance are identical to the elements of an offense defined by State or federal law.

The fact that a State or federal law, standing alone, makes a given act, omission, or condition unlawful shall not preclude city ordinances requiring a higher standard of conduct or condition.

## § 160A-175. Enforcement of ordinances.

(a)    A city shall have power to impose fines and penalties for violation of its ordinances, and may secure injunctions and abatement orders to further insure compliance with its ordinances as provided by this section.

(b)    Unless the Council shall otherwise provide, violation of a city ordinance is a misdemeanor or infraction as provided by G.S. 14-4. An ordinance may provide by express statement that the maximum fine, term of imprisonment, or infraction penalty to be imposed for a violation is some amount of money or number of days less than the maximum imposed by G.S. 14-4.

(c)    An ordinance may provide that violation shall subject the offender to a civil penalty to be recovered by the city in a civil action in the nature of debt if the offender does not pay the penalty within a prescribed period of time after he has been cited for violation of the ordinance.

(c1)    An ordinance may provide for the recovery of a civil penalty by the city for violation of the fire prevention code of the State Building Code as authorized under G.S. 143-139.

(d)    An ordinance may provide that it may be enforced by an appropriate equitable remedy issuing from a court of competent jurisdiction. In such case, the General Court of Justice shall have jurisdiction to issue such orders as may be appropriate, and it shall not be a defense to the application of the city for equitable relief that there is an adequate remedy at law.

(e)    An ordinance that makes unlawful a condition existing upon or use made of real property may be enforced by injunction and order of abatement, and the General Court of Justice shall have jurisdiction to issue such orders. When a violation of such an ordinance occurs the city may apply to the appropriate division of the General Court of Justice for a mandatory or prohibitory injunction and order of abatement commanding the defendant to correct the unlawful condition upon or cease the unlawful use of the property. The action shall be governed in all respects by the laws and rules governing civil proceedings, including the Rules of Civil Procedure in general and Rule 65 in particular.

In addition to an injunction, the court may enter an order of abatement as a part of the judgment in the cause. An order of abatement may direct that buildings or other structures on the property be closed, demolished, or removed; that fixtures, furniture, or other movable property be removed from buildings on the property; that grass and weeds be cut; that improvements or repairs be made; or that any other action be taken that is necessary to bring the property into compliance with the ordinance. If the defendant fails or refuses to comply with an injunction or with an order of abatement within the time allowed by the court, he may be cited for contempt, and the city may execute the order of abatement. The city shall have a lien on the property for the cost of executing an order of abatement in the nature of a mechanic's and materialman's lien. The defendant may secure cancellation of an order of abatement by paying all costs of the proceedings and posting a bond for compliance with the order. The bond shall be given with sureties approved by the clerk of superior court in an amount approved by the judge before whom the matter is heard and shall be conditioned on the defendant's full compliance with the terms of the order of abatement within a time fixed by the judge. Cancellation of an order of abatement shall not suspend or cancel an injunction issued in conjunction therewith.

(f)    Subject to the express terms of the ordinance, a city ordinance may be enforced by any one, all, or a combination of the remedies authorized and prescribed by this section.

(g)    A city ordinance may provide, when appropriate, that each day's continuing violation shall be a separate and distinct offense.

## Minimum Housing Code

*Chapter 153A, Article 18: Planning and Regulation of Development (counties)*

### § 153A-323. Procedure for adopting, amending, or repealing ordinances under this Article and Chapter 160A, Article 19.

(a)　Before adopting, amending, or repealing any ordinance authorized by this Article or Chapter 160A, Article 19, the board of commissioners shall hold a public hearing on the ordinance or amendment. The board shall cause notice of the hearing to be published once a week for two successive calendar weeks. The notice shall be published the first time not less than 10 days nor more than 25 days before the date fixed for the hearing. In computing such period, the day of publication is not to be included but the day of the hearing shall be included.

(b)　If the adoption or modification of the ordinance would result in changes to the zoning map or would change or affect the permitted uses of land located five miles or less from the perimeter boundary of a military base, the board of commissioners shall provide written notice of the proposed changes by certified mail, return receipt requested, to the commander of the military base not less than 10 days nor more than 25 days before the date fixed for the public hearing. If the military provides comments or analysis regarding the compatibility of the proposed ordinance or amendment with military operations at the base, the board of commissioners shall take the comments and analysis into consideration before making a final determination on the ordinance.

*Chapter 160A, Article 19: Planning and Regulation of Development (cities)*
*Part 1. General Provisions*

### § 160A-364. Procedure for adopting, amending, or repealing ordinances under Article.

(a)　Before adopting, amending, or repealing any ordinance authorized by this Article, the city council shall hold a public hearing on it. A notice of the public hearing shall be given once a week for two successive calendar weeks in a newspaper having general circulation in the area. The notice shall be published the first time not less than 10 days nor more than 25 days before the date fixed for the hearing. In computing such period, the day of publication is not to be included but the day of the hearing shall be included.

(b)　If the adoption or modification of the ordinance would result in changes to the zoning map or would change or affect the permitted uses of land located five miles or less from the perimeter boundary of a military base, the governing body of the local government shall provide written notice of the proposed changes by certified mail, return receipt requested, to the commander of the military base not less than 10 days nor more than 25 days before the date fixed for the public hearing. If the military provides comments or analysis regarding the compatibility of the proposed ordinance or amendment with military operations at the base, the governing body of the local government shall take the comments and analysis into consideration before making a final determination on the ordinance.

## Part 6. Minimum Housing Standards
### § 160A-441. Exercise of police power authorized.

It is hereby found and declared that the existence and occupation of dwellings in this State that are unfit for human habitation are inimical to the welfare and dangerous and injurious to the health, safety and morals of the people of this State, and that a public necessity exists for the repair, closing or demolition of such dwellings. Whenever any city or county of this State finds that there exists in the city or county dwellings that are unfit for human habitation due to dilapidation, defects increasing the hazards of fire, accidents or other calamities, lack of ventilation, light or sanitary facilities, or due to other conditions rendering the dwellings unsafe or unsanitary, or dangerous or detrimental to the health, safety, morals, or otherwise inimical to the welfare of the residents of the city or county, power is hereby conferred upon the city or county to exercise its police powers to repair, close or demolish the dwellings in the manner herein provided. No ordinance enacted by the governing body of a county pursuant to this Part shall be applicable within the corporate limits of any city unless the city council of the city has by resolution expressly given its approval thereto.

In addition to the exercise of police power authorized herein, any city may by ordinance provide for the repair, closing or demolition of any abandoned structure which the city council finds to be a health or safety hazard as a result of the attraction of insects or rodents, conditions creating a fire hazard, dangerous conditions constituting a threat to children or frequent use by vagrants as living quarters in the absence of sanitary facilities. Such ordinance, if adopted, may provide for the repair, closing or demolition of such structure pursuant to the same provisions and procedures as are prescribed herein for the repair, closing or demolition of dwellings found to be unfit for human habitation.

## § 160A-442. Definitions.

The following terms shall have the meanings whenever used or referred to as indicated when used in this Part unless a different meaning clearly appears from the context:

(1)    "City" means any incorporated city or any county.

(2)    "Dwelling" means any building, structure, manufactured home or mobile home, or part thereof, used and occupied for human habitation or intended to be so used, and includes any outhouses and appurtenances belonging thereto or usually enjoyed therewith, except that it does not include any manufactured home or mobile home, which is used solely for a seasonal vacation purpose.

(3)    "Governing body" means the council, board of commissioners, or other legislative body, charged with governing a city or county.

(3a)    "Manufactured home" or "mobile home" means a structure as defined in G.S. 143-145(7).

(4)    "Owner" means the holder of the title in fee simple and every mortgagee of record.

(5)    "Parties in interest" means all individuals, associations and corporations who have interests of record in a dwelling and any who are in possession thereof.

(6)    "Public authority" means any housing authority or any officer who is in charge of any department or branch of the government of the city, county, or State relating to health, fire, building regulations, or other activities concerning dwellings in the city.

(7)    "Public officer" means the officer or officers who are authorized by ordinances adopted hereunder to exercise the powers prescribed by the ordinances and by this Part.

## § 160A-443. Ordinance authorized as to repair, closing, and demolition; order of public officer.

Upon the adoption of an ordinance finding that dwelling conditions of the character described in G.S. 160A-441 exist within a city, the governing body of the city is hereby authorized to adopt and enforce ordinances relating to dwellings within the city's territorial jurisdiction that are unfit for human habitation. These ordinances shall include the following provisions:

(1)    That a public officer be designated or appointed to exercise the powers prescribed by the ordinance.

(2)    That whenever a petition is filed with the public officer by a public authority or by at least five residents of the city charging that any dwelling is unfit for human habitation or whenever it appears to the public officer (on his own motion) that any dwelling is unfit for human habitation, the public officer shall, if his preliminary investigation discloses a basis for such charges, issue and cause to be served upon the owner of and parties in interest in such dwellings a complaint stating the charges in that respect and containing a notice that a hearing will be held before the public officer (or his designated agent) at a place within the county in which the property is located fixed not less than 10 days nor more than 30 days after the serving of the complaint; that the owner and parties in interest shall be given the right to file an answer to the complaint and to appear in person, or otherwise, and give testimony at the place and time fixed in the complaint; and that the rules of evidence prevailing in courts of law or equity shall not be controlling in hearings before the public officer.

(3)    That if, after notice and hearing, the public officer determines that the dwelling under consideration is unfit for human habitation, he shall state in writing his findings of fact in support of that determination and shall issue and cause to be served upon the owner thereof an order,

    a.    If the repair, alteration or improvement of the dwelling can be made at a reasonable cost in relation to the value of the dwelling (the ordinance of the city may fix a certain percentage of this value as being reasonable), requiring the owner, within the time specified, to repair, alter or improve the dwelling in order to render it fit for human habitation. The order may require that the property be vacated and closed only if continued occupancy during the time allowed for repair will present a significant threat of bodily harm, taking into account the nature of the necessary repairs, alterations, or improvements; the current state of the property; and any additional risks due to the presence and capacity of minors under the age of 18 or occupants with physical or mental disabilities.

The order shall state that the failure to make timely repairs as directed in the order shall make the dwelling subject to the issuance of an unfit order under subdivision (4) of this section; or

b.  If the repair, alteration or improvement of the dwelling cannot be made at a reasonable cost in relation to the value of the dwelling (the ordinance of the city may fix a certain percentage of this value as being reasonable), requiring the owner, within the time specified in the order, to remove or demolish such dwelling. However, notwithstanding any other provision of law, if the dwelling is located in a historic district of the city and the Historic District Commission determines, after a public hearing as provided by ordinance, that the dwelling is of particular significance or value toward maintaining the character of the district, and the dwelling has not been condemned as unsafe, the order may require that the dwelling be vacated and closed consistent with G.S. 160A-400.14(a).

(4)  That, if the owner fails to comply with an order to repair, alter or improve or to vacate and close the dwelling, the public officer may cause the dwelling to be repaired, altered or improved or to be vacated and closed; that the public officer may cause to be posted on the main entrance of any dwelling so closed, a placard with the following words: "This building is unfit for human habitation; the use or occupation of this building for human habitation is prohibited and unlawful." Occupation of a building so posted shall constitute a Class 1 misdemeanor. The duties of the public officer set forth in this subdivision shall not be exercised until the governing body shall have by ordinance ordered the public officer to proceed to effectuate the purpose of this Article with respect to the particular property or properties which the public officer shall have found to be unfit for human habitation and which property or properties shall be described in the ordinance. This ordinance shall be recorded in the office of the register of deeds in the county wherein the property or properties are

located and shall be indexed in the name of the property owner in the grantor index.

(5)     That, if the owner fails to comply with an order to remove or demolish the dwelling, the public officer may cause such dwelling to be removed or demolished. The duties of the public officer set forth in this subdivision shall not be exercised until the governing body shall have by ordinance ordered the public officer to proceed to effectuate the purpose of this Article with respect to the particular property or properties which the public officer shall have found to be unfit for human habitation and which property or properties shall be described in the ordinance. No such ordinance shall be adopted to require demolition of a dwelling until the owner has first been given a reasonable opportunity to bring it into conformity with the housing code. This ordinance shall be recorded in the office of the register of deeds in the county wherein the property or properties are located and shall be indexed in the name of the property owner in the grantor index.

(5a)    If the governing body shall have adopted an ordinance as provided in subdivision (4) of this section, or the public officer shall have:

a.      In a municipality located in counties which have a population in excess of 71,000 by the last federal census (including the entirety of any municipality located in more than one county at least one county of which has a population in excess of 71,000), other than municipalities with a population in excess of 190,000 by the last federal census, issued an order, ordering a dwelling to be repaired or vacated and closed, as provided in subdivision (3)a, and if the dwelling has been vacated and closed for a period of one year pursuant to the ordinance or order;

b.      In a municipality with a population in excess of 190,000 by the last federal census, commenced proceedings under the substandard housing regulations regarding a dwelling to be repaired or vacated and closed, as provided in subdivision (3) a., and if the dwelling has been vacated and closed for a period of one year pursuant to the ordinance or after such proceedings have commenced,

then if the governing body shall find that the owner has abandoned the intent and purpose to repair, alter or improve the dwelling in order to render it fit for human habitation and that the continuation of the dwelling in its vacated and closed status would be inimical to the health, safety, morals and welfare of the municipality in that the dwelling would continue to deteriorate, would create a fire and safety hazard, would be a threat to children and vagrants, would attract persons intent on criminal activities, would cause or contribute to blight and the deterioration of property values in the area, and would render unavailable property and a dwelling which might otherwise have been made available to ease the persistent shortage of decent and affordable housing in this State, then in such circumstances, the governing body may, after the expiration of such one year period, enact an ordinance and serve such ordinance on the owner, setting forth the following:

a.    If it is determined that the repair of the dwelling to render it fit for human habitation can be made at a cost not exceeding fifty percent (50%) of the then current value of the dwelling, the ordinance shall require that the owner either repair or demolish and remove the dwelling within 90 days; or

b.    If it is determined that the repair of the dwelling to render it fit for human habitation cannot be made at a cost not exceeding fifty percent (50%) of the then current value of the dwelling, the ordinance shall require the owner to demolish and remove the dwelling within 90 days.

This ordinance shall be recorded in the Office of the Register of Deeds in the county wherein the property or properties are located and shall be indexed in the name of the property owner in the grantor index. If the owner fails to comply with this ordinance, the public officer shall effectuate the purpose of the ordinance.

This subdivision only applies to municipalities located in counties which have a population in excess of 71,000 by the last federal census (including the entirety of any municipality located in more than one county at least one county of which has a population in excess of 71,000).

[This subdivision does not apply to the local government units listed in subdivision (5b) of this section.]

(5b)    If the governing body shall have adopted an ordinance as provided in subdivision (4) of this section, or the public officer shall have:

a.    In a municipality other than municipalities with a population in excess of 190,000 by the last federal census, issued an order, ordering a dwelling to be repaired or vacated and closed, as provided in subdivision (3)a, and if the dwelling has been vacated and closed for a period of one year pursuant to the ordinance or order;

b.    In a municipality with a population in excess of 190,000 by the last federal census, commenced proceedings under the substandard housing regulations regarding a dwelling to be repaired or vacated and closed, as provided in subdivision (3)a., and if the dwelling has been vacated and closed for a period of one year pursuant to the ordinance or after such proceedings have commenced,

then if the governing body shall find that the owner has abandoned the intent and purpose to repair, alter or improve the dwelling in order to render it fit for human habitation and that the continuation of the dwelling in its vacated and closed status would be inimical to the health, safety, morals and welfare of the municipality in that the dwelling would continue to deteriorate, would create a fire and safety hazard, would be a threat to children and vagrants, would attract persons intent on criminal activities, would cause or contribute to blight and the deterioration of property values in the area, and would render unavailable property and a dwelling which might otherwise have been made available to ease the persistent shortage of decent and affordable housing in this State, then in such circumstances, the governing body may, after the expiration of such one year period, enact an ordinance and serve such ordinance on the owner, setting forth the following:

    a.      If it is determined that the repair of the dwelling to render it fit for human habitation can be made at a cost not exceeding fifty percent (50%) of the then current value of the dwelling, the ordinance shall require that the owner either repair or demolish and remove the dwelling within 90 days; or

    b.      If it is determined that the repair of the dwelling to render it fit for human habitation cannot be made at a cost not exceeding fifty percent (50%) of the then current value of the dwelling, the ordinance shall require the owner to demolish and remove the dwelling within 90 days.

This ordinance shall be recorded in the Office of the Register of Deeds in the county wherein the property or properties are located and shall be indexed in the name of the property owner in the grantor index. If the owner fails to comply with this ordinance, the public officer shall effectuate the purpose of the ordinance.

This subdivision applies to the Cities of Eden, Lumberton, Roanoke Rapids, and Whiteville, to the municipalities in Lee County, and the Towns of Bethel, Farmville, Newport, and Waynesville only.

(6)    Liens. –

    a.      That the amount of the cost of repairs, alterations or improvements, or vacating and closing, or removal or demolition by the public officer shall be a lien against the real property upon which the cost was incurred, which lien shall be filed, have the same priority, and be collected as the lien for special assessment provided in Article 10 of this Chapter.

    b.      If the real property upon which the cost was incurred is located in an incorporated city, then the amount of the cost is also a lien on any other real property of the owner located within the city limits or within one mile thereof except for the owner's primary residence. The additional lien provided in this sub-subdivision is inferior to all prior liens and shall be collected as a money judgment.

c.    If the dwelling is removed or demolished by the public officer, he shall sell the materials of the dwelling, and any personal property, fixtures or appurtenances found in or attached to the dwelling, and shall credit the proceeds of the sale against the cost of the removal or demolition and any balance remaining shall be deposited in the superior court by the public officer, shall be secured in a manner directed by the court, and shall be disbursed by the court to the persons found to be entitled thereto by final order or decree of the court. Nothing in this section shall be construed to impair or limit in any way the power of the city to define and declare nuisances and to cause their removal or abatement by summary proceedings, or otherwise.

(7)    If any occupant fails to comply with an order to vacate a dwelling, the public officer may file a civil action in the name of the city to remove such occupant. The action to vacate the dwelling shall be in the nature of summary ejectment and shall be commenced by filing a complaint naming as parties-defendant any person occupying such dwelling. The clerk of superior court shall issue a summons requiring the defendant to appear before a magistrate at a certain time, date and place not to exceed 10 days from the issuance of the summons to answer the complaint. The summons and complaint shall be served as provided in G.S. 42-29. The summons shall be returned according to its tenor, and if on its return it appears to have been duly served, and if at the hearing the public officer produces a certified copy of an ordinance adopted by the governing body pursuant to subdivision (5) authorizing the officer to proceed to vacate the occupied dwelling, the magistrate shall enter judgment ordering that the premises be vacated and that all persons be removed. The judgment ordering that the dwelling be vacated shall be enforced in the same manner as the judgment for summary ejectment entered under G.S. 42-30. An appeal from

any judgment entered hereunder by the magistrate may be taken as provided in G.S. 7A-228, and the execution of such judgment may be stayed as provided in G.S. 7A-227. An action to remove an occupant of a dwelling who is a tenant of the owner may not be in the nature of a summary ejectment proceeding pursuant to this paragraph unless such occupant was served with notice at least 30 days before the filing of the summary ejectment proceeding that the governing body has ordered the public officer to proceed to exercise his duties under subdivisions (4) and (5) of this section to vacate and close or remove and demolish the dwelling.

(8) That whenever a determination is made pursuant to subdivision (3) of this section that a dwelling must be vacated and closed, or removed or demolished, under the provisions of this section, notice of the order shall be given by first-class mail to any organization involved in providing or restoring dwellings for affordable housing that has filed a written request for such notices. A minimum period of 45 days from the mailing of such notice shall be given before removal or demolition by action of the public officer, to allow the opportunity for any organization to negotiate with the owner to make repairs, lease, or purchase the property for the purpose of providing affordable housing. The public officer or clerk shall certify the mailing of the notices, and the certification shall be conclusive in the absence of fraud. Only an organization that has filed a written request for such notices may raise the issue of failure to mail such notices, and the sole remedy shall be an order requiring the public officer to wait 45 days before causing removal or demolition.

## § 160A-443.1. Heat source required.

(a) A city shall, by ordinance, require that by January 1, 2000, every dwelling unit leased as rental property within the city shall have, at a minimum, a central or electric heating system or sufficient chimneys, flues, or gas vents, with heating appliances connected, so as to heat at least one habitable room, excluding the kitchen, to a minimum temperature of 68 degrees Fahrenheit measured three feet above the floor with an outside temperature of 20 degrees Fahrenheit.

(b)     If a dwelling unit contains a heating system or heating appliances that meet the requirements of subsection (a) of this section, the owner of the dwelling unit shall not be required to install a new heating system or heating appliances, but the owner shall be required to maintain the existing heating system or heating appliances in a good and safe working condition. Otherwise, the owner of the dwelling unit shall install a heating system or heating appliances that meet the requirements of subsection (a) of this section and shall maintain the heating system or heating appliances in a good and safe working condition.

(c)     Portable kerosene heaters are not acceptable as a permanent source of heat as required by subsection (a) of this section but may be used as a supplementary source in single family dwellings and duplex units. An owner who has complied with subsection (a) shall not be held in violation of this section where an occupant of a dwelling unit uses a kerosene heater as a primary source of heat.

(d)     This section applies only to cities with a population of 200,000 or over, according to the most recent decennial federal census.

(e)     Nothing in this section shall be construed as:

   (1)     Diminishing the rights of or remedies available to any tenant under a lease agreement, statute, or at common law; or

   (2)     Prohibiting a city from adopting an ordinance with more stringent heating requirements than provided for by this section.

### § 160A-444. Standards.

An ordinance adopted by a city under this Part shall provide that the public officer may determine that a dwelling is unfit for human habitation if he finds that conditions exist in the dwelling that render it dangerous or injurious to the health, safety or morals of the occupants of the dwelling, the occupants of neighboring dwellings, or other residents of the city. Defective conditions may include the following (without limiting the generality of the foregoing): defects therein increasing the hazards of fire, accident, or other calamities; lack of adequate ventilation, light, or sanitary facilities; dilapidation; disrepair; structural defects; uncleanliness. The ordinances may provide additional standards to guide the public officers, or his agents, in determining the fitness of a dwelling for human habitation.

### § 160A-445. Service of complaints and orders.

(a)     Complaints or orders issued by a public officer pursuant to an ordinance adopted under this Part shall be served upon persons either personally or by registered or certified mail. When service is made by registered or certified mail, a copy of the complaint or order may also be sent by regular mail. Service shall be deemed sufficient if the registered or certified mail is unclaimed or refused, but the regular mail is not returned by the post office within 10 days after the mailing. If regular mail is used, a notice of the pending proceedings shall be posted in a conspicuous place on the premises affected.

(a1)     If the identities of any owners or the whereabouts of persons are unknown and cannot be ascertained by the public officer in the exercise of reasonable diligence, or, if the owners are known but have refused to accept service by registered or certified mail, and the public officer makes an affidavit to that effect, then the serving of the complaint or order upon the owners or other persons may be made by publication in a newspaper having general circulation in the city at least once no later than the time at which personal service would be required under the provisions of this Part. When service is made by publication, a notice of the pending proceedings shall be posted in a conspicuous place on the premises thereby affected.

(b)     Repealed by Session Laws 1997, c. 201, s. 1.

### § 160A-446. Remedies.

(a)     The governing body may provide for the creation and organization of a housing appeals board to which appeals may be taken from any decision or order of the public officer, or may provide for such appeals to be heard and determined by its zoning board of adjustment.

(b)     The housing appeals board, if created, shall consist of five members to serve for three-year staggered terms. It shall have the power to elect its own officers, to fix the times and places for its meetings, to adopt necessary rules of procedure, and to adopt other rules and regulations for the proper discharge of its duties. It shall keep an accurate record of all its proceedings.

(c)     An appeal from any decision or order of the public officer may be taken by any person aggrieved thereby or by any officer, board or commission of the city. Any appeal from the public officer shall be taken within 10 days from the rendering of the decision or service of the order by filing with the public officer and with the board a notice of appeal which shall specify the grounds upon which the appeal is based. Upon the filing of any notice of appeal, the public officer shall forthwith transmit to the board all the papers constituting the record upon which the decision appealed from was made. When an appeal is from a decision of the public officer refusing to allow the person aggrieved thereby to do any act, his decision shall remain in force until modified or reversed. When any appeal is from a decision of the public officer requiring the person aggrieved to do any act, the appeal shall have the effect of suspending the requirement until the hearing by the board, unless the public officer certifies to the board, after the notice of appeal is filed with him, that because of facts stated in the certificate (a copy of which shall be furnished the appellant), a suspension of his requirement would cause imminent peril to life or property. In that case the requirement shall not be suspended except by a restraining order, which may be granted for due cause shown upon not less than one day's written notice to the public officer, by the board, or by a court of record upon petition made pursuant to subsection (f) of this section.

(d)     The appeals board shall fix a reasonable time for hearing appeals, shall give due notice to the parties, and shall render its decision within a reasonable time. Any party may appear in person or by agent or attorney. The board may reverse or affirm, wholly or partly, or may modify the decision or order appealed from, and may make any decision and order that in its opinion ought to be made in the matter, and to that end it shall have all the powers of the public officer, but the concurring vote of four members of the board shall be necessary to reverse or modify any decision or order of the public officer. The board shall have power also in passing upon appeals, when practical difficulties or unnecessary hardships would result from carrying out the strict letter of the ordinance, to adapt the application of the ordinance to the necessities of the case to the end that the spirit of the ordinance shall be observed, public safety and welfare secured, and substantial justice done.

(e)     Every decision of the board shall be subject to review by proceedings in the nature of certiorari instituted within 15 days of the decision of the board, but not otherwise.

(f)     Any person aggrieved by an order issued by the public officer or a decision rendered by the board may petition the superior court for an injunction restraining the public officer from carrying out the order or decision and the court may, upon such petition, issue a temporary injunction restraining the public officer pending a final disposition of the cause. The petition shall be filed within 30 days after issuance of the order or rendering of the decision. Hearings shall be had by the court on a petition within 20 days, and shall be given preference over other matters on the court's calendar. The court shall hear and determine the issues raised and shall enter such final order or decree as law and justice may require. It shall not be necessary to file bond in any amount before obtaining a temporary injunction under this subsection.

(g)     If any dwelling is erected, constructed, altered, repaired, converted, maintained, or used in violation of this Part or of any ordinance or code adopted under authority of this Part or any valid order or decision of the public officer or board made pursuant to any ordinance or code adopted under authority of this Part, the public officer or board may institute any appropriate action or proceedings to prevent the unlawful erection, construction, reconstruction, alteration or use, to restrain, correct or abate the violation, to prevent the occupancy of the dwelling, or to prevent any illegal act, conduct or use in or about the premises of the dwelling.

### § 160A-447. Compensation to owners of condemned property.

Nothing in this Part shall be construed as preventing the owner or owners of any property from receiving just compensation for the taking of property by the power of eminent domain under the laws of this State, nor as permitting any property to be condemned or destroyed except in accordance with the police power of the State.

### § 160A-448. Additional powers of public officer.

An ordinance adopted by the governing body of the city may authorize the public officer to exercise any powers necessary or convenient to carry out and effectuate the purpose and provisions of this Part, including the following powers in addition to others herein granted:

    (1)    To investigate the dwelling conditions in the city in order to determine which dwellings therein are unfit for human habitations;

    (2)    To administer oaths, affirmations, examine witnesses and receive evidence;

    (3)    To enter upon premises for the purpose of making examinations in a manner that will do the least possible inconvenience to the persons in possession;

    (4)    To appoint and fix the duties of officers, agents and employees necessary to carry out the purposes of the ordinances; and

    (5)    To delegate any of his functions and powers under the ordinance to other officers and other agents.

### § 160A-449. Administration of ordinance.

The governing body of any city adopting an ordinance under this Part shall, as soon as possible thereafter, prepare an estimate of the annual expenses or costs to provide the equipment, personnel and supplies necessary for periodic examinations and investigations of the dwellings in the city for the purpose of determining the fitness of dwellings for human habitation, and for the enforcement and administration of its ordinances adopted under this Part. The city is authorized to make appropriations from its revenues necessary for this purpose and may accept and apply grants or donations to assist it in carrying out the provisions of the ordinances.

### § 160A-450. Supplemental nature of Part.

Nothing in this Part shall be construed to abrogate or impair the powers of the courts or of any department of any city to enforce any provisions of its charter or its ordinances or regulations, nor to prevent or punish violations thereof; and the powers conferred by this Part shall be in addition and supplemental to the powers conferred by any other law.

# Appendix 4
# Location of Chapter 160D Provisions in Prior Statutes

Updated to August 17, 2020

| CHAPTER 160D | CHAPTER 153A | CHAPTER 160A |
|---|---|---|
| **ARTICLE 1. General Provisions** | | |
| §160D-101. Application. | -- | -- |
| §160D-102. Definitions. | 153A-344.1(b) | 160A-1(3) |
| | 153A-349.2 | 160A-385(a)(2) |
| | | 160A-385.1(b) |
| | | 160A-393(a) |
| | | 160A-400.9 |
| | | 160A-400.21 |
| | | 160A-442 |
| §160D-103. Unified development ordinance. | 153A-322(d) | 160A-363(d) |
| §160D-104. Development approvals run with the land. | -- | -- |
| §160D-105. Maps. | -- | -- |
| §160D-106. Refund of illegal fees. | 153A-324(b) | 160A-363(e) |
| §160D-107. Moratoria. | 153A-340(h) | 160A-381(e) |
| §160D-108. Permit choice and vested rights. | 153A-320.1 | 160A-360.1 |
| | 153A-344 | 160A-385 |
| | 153A-344.1 | 160A-385.1 |
| §160D-108.1. Vested rights–Site specific vesting plans. | 153A-344.1 | 160A-385.1 |
| §160D-109. Conflicts of interest. | 153A-340(g) | 160A-381(d) |
| | 153A-355 | 160A-388(e) |
| | | 160A-415 |
| §160D-110. Chapter construction. | -- | -- |
| §160D-111. Effect on prior laws. | 153A-2 | 160A-2 |
| | | 160A-5 |
| | | 160A-366 |

## ARTICLE 2. Planning and Development Regulation Jurisdiction

| | | |
|---|---|---|
| §160D-201. Planning and development regulation jurisdiction. | 153A-320 | 160A-360 |
| §160D-202. Municipal extra territorial jurisdiction. | -- | 160-360 |
| §160D-203. Split jurisdiction. | -- | -- |
| §160D-204. Pending jurisdiction. | -- | -- |

## ARTICLE 3. Boards and Organizational Arrangements

| | | |
|---|---|---|
| §160D-301. Planning boards. | 153A-361 | 160A-321 |
| §160D-302. Boards of adjustment. | -- | 160A-388 |
| §160D-303. Historic preservation commission. | -- | 160A-400.7 |
| §160D-304. Appearance commission. | -- | 160A-451 |
| §160D-305. Housing appeals board. | -- | 160A-446 |
| §160D-306. Other advisory boards. | -- | -- |
| §160D-307. Extra territorial representation on boards. | -- | 160A-362 |
| §160D-308. Rules of procedure. | -- | -- |
| §160D-309. Oath of office. | -- | -- |
| §160D-310. Appointments to boards. | -- | -- |

## ARTICLE 4. Administration, Enforcement, and Appeals

| | | |
|---|---|---|
| §160D-401. Application. | -- | -- |
| §160D-402. Administrative staff. | 153A-351<br>153A-352<br>153A-353<br>153A-354 | 160A-411<br>160A-412<br>160A-413<br>160A-414 |
| § 160D-403. Administrative development approvals and determinations. | 153A-357<br>153A-358<br>153A-359<br>153A-360<br>153A-362<br>153A-363 | 160A-388<br>160A-417<br>160A-418<br>160A-419<br>160A-420<br>160A-422<br>160A-423 |
| §160D-404. Enforcement. | 153A-324<br>153A-361 | 160A-365<br>160A-389<br>160A-400.11<br>160A-421 |
| §160D-405. Appeals of administrative decisions. | -- | 160A-388 |
| §160D-406. Quasi-judicial procedure. | -- | 160A-388 |

## ARTICLE 5. Planning

| | | |
|---|---|---|
| §160D-501. Plans. | -- | -- |
| §160D-502. Grants, contracts, and technical assistance. | 153A-322 | 160A-363 |
| §160D-503. Coordination of planning. | -- | -- |

## ARTICLE 6. Development Regulation

| | | |
|---|---|---|
| §160D-601. Procedure for adopting, amending, or repealing development regulations. | 153A-323, 153A-343 | 160A-364, 160A-384 |
| §160D-602. Notice of hearing on proposed zoning map amendments. | 153A-343 | 160A-384 |
| §160D-603. Citizen comments. | -- | 160A-385 160A-386 |
| §160D-604. Planning board review and comments. | 153A-341 153A-344 | 160A-383 160A-387 |
| §160D-605. Governing board statement. | 153A-341 153A-342 | 160A-382 160A-383 |

## ARTICLE 7. Zoning Regulation

| | | |
|---|---|---|
| §160D-701. Purposes. | 153A-341 | 160A-383 |
| §160D-702. Grant of power. | 153A-340 | 160A-381 |
| §160D-703. Zoning districts. | 153A-342 | 160A-382 |
| §160D-704. Incentives. | 153A-340 | 160A-381 160A-383.4 |
| §160D-705. Quasi-judicial zoning decisions. | 153A-340 | 160A-381 160A-388 |
| §160D-706. Zoning conflicts with other development standards. | 153A-346 | 160A-390 |

## ARTICLE 8. Subdivision Regulation

| | | |
|---|---|---|
| §160D-801. Authority. | 153A-330 | 160A-371 |
| §160D-802. Applicability. | 153A-335 | 160A-376 |
| §160D-803. Review process, filing, and recording of subdivision plats. | 153A-332 | 160A-373 |
| §160D-804. Contents and requirements of regulation. | 153A-331 | 160A-372 |
| §160D-804.1. Performance guarantees | 153A-331 | 160A-372 |
| §160D-805. Notice of new subdivision fees and fee increases; public comment period. | 153A-102.1 | 160A-4.1 |
| §160D-806. Effect of plat approval on dedications. | 153A-333 | 160A-374 |
| §160D-807. Penalties for transferring lots in unapproved subdivisions. | 153A-334 | 160A-375 |
| 1§60D-808. Appeals of decisions on subdivision plats. | 153A-336 | 160A-377 |

## ARTICLE 9. Regulation of Particular Uses and Areas

### Part1. Particular Land Uses

| | | |
|---|---|---|
| §160D-901. Regulation of particular uses and areas. | | |
| §160D-902. Adult businesses. | -- | 160A-181.1 |
| §160D-903. Agricultural uses. | 153A-340 | 160A-360 160A-383.2 |
| §160D-904.Airportzoning. | -- | -- |
| §160D-905. Amateur radio antennas. | 153A-341.2 | 160A-383.3 |
| §160D-906. Beehives. | -- | -- |
| §160D-907. Family care homes. | -- | 168-20 168-21 168-22 |
| §160D-908. Fence wraps. | 153A-340 | 160A-381 |
| §160D-909. Fraternities and sororities. | 153A-340 | 160A-382 |
| §160D-910. Manufactured homes. | 153A-341.1 | 160A-383.1 |
| §160D-911. Modular homes. | -- | -- |
| §160D-912. Outdoor advertising. | 153A-143 | 160A-199 |
| §160D-913. Public buildings. | 153A-347 | 160A-392 |
| §160D-914. Solar collectors. | 153A-144 | 160A-201 |
| §160D-915. Temporary health care structures. | 153A-341.3 | 160A-383.5 |
| §160D-916. Streets and transportation. | -- | 160A-458.4 |

### Part 2. Environmental Regulations

| | | |
|---|---|---|
| §160D-920. Local environmental regulations. | -- | -- |
| §160D-921. Forestry activities. | 153A-452 | 160A-458.5 |
| §160D-922. Erosion and sedimentation control. | | 160A-458 |
| §160D-923. Flood plain regulations. | -- | 160A-458.1 |
| §160D-924. Mountain ridge protection. | 153A-448 | 160A-458.2 |
| §160D-925. Storm water control. | 153A-454 | 160A-459 |
| §160D-926. Water supply watershed management. | -- | -- |

### Part 3. Wireless Telecommunication Facilities

| | | |
|---|---|---|
| §160D-930. Purpose and compliance with federal law. | 153A-349.50 | 160A-400.50 |
| §160D-931. Definitions. | 153A-349.51 | 160A-400.51 |
| §160D-932. Local authority. | 153A-349.51A | 160A-400.51A |
| §160D-933. Construction of new wireless support structures or substantial modifications of wireless support structures. | 153A-349.52 | 160A-400.52 |
| §160D-934. Collocation and eligible facilities requests of wireless support structures. | 153A-349.53 | 160A-400.53 |

| CHAPTER 160D | CHAPTER 153A | CHAPTER 160A |
|---|---|---|
| §160D-935. Collocation of small wireless facilities. | -- | 160A-400.54 |
| §160D-936. Use of public rights-of-way. | -- | 160A-400.55 |
| §160D-937. Access to city utility poles to install small wireless facilities. | -- | 160A-400.56 |
| §160D-938. Applicability. | -- | 160A-400.57 |
| *Part 4. Historic Preservation* | | |
| §160D-940. Legislative findings. | -- | 160A-400.1 |
| §160D-941. Historic preservation commission. | -- | 160A-400.7 |
| §160D-942. Powers of the historic preservation commission. | -- | 160A-400.8 |
| §160D-943. Appropriations. | -- | 160A-400.12 |
| §160D-944. Designation of historic districts. | -- | 160A-400.3 160A-400.4 |
| §160D-945. Designation of landmarks. | -- | 160A-400.5 |
| §160D-946. Required landmark designation procedure. | -- | 160A-400.6 |
| §160D-947. Certificate of appropriateness required. | -- | 160A-400.9 |
| §160D-948. Certain changes not prohibited. | -- | 160A-400.13 |
| § 160D-949. Delay in demolition of landmarks and buildings within historic district. | -- | 160A-400.14 |
| §160D-950. Demolition by neglect in contributing structures outside local historic districts. | -- | 160A-400.15 |
| §160D-951. Conflict with other laws. | -- | 160A-400.10 |
| *Part 5. Community Appearance Commission* | | |
| §160D-960. Powers and duties of commission. | -- | 160A-452 |
| §160D-961. Staff services; advisory board. | -- | 160A-453 |
| §160D-962. Annual report. | -- | 160A-454 |
| §160D-963. Receipt and expenditure of funds. | -- | 160A-455 |

## ARTICLE 10. Development Agreements

| CHAPTER 160D | CHAPTER 153A | CHAPTER 160A |
|---|---|---|
| §160D-1001. Authorization. | 153A-349.1 | 160A-400.20 |
| §160D-1002. Definitions. | 153A-349.2 | 160A-400.21 |
| §160D-1003. Approval of governing board required. | 153A-349.3 | 160A-400.22 |
| §160D-1004. Size and duration. | 153A-349.4 | 160A-400.23 |
| §160D-1005. Hearing. | 153A-349.5 | 160A-400.24 |
| §160D-1006. Content and modification. | 153A-349.6 | 160A-400.25 |
| §160D-1007. Vesting. | 153A-349.7 | 160A-400.26 |
| §160D-1008. Breach and cure. | 153A-349.8 | 160A-400.27 |
| §160D-1009. Amendment or termination. | 153A-349.9 | 160A-400.28 |

| CHAPTER 160D | CHAPTER 153A | CHAPTER 160A |
|---|---|---|
| §160D-1010. Change of jurisdiction. | 153A-349.10 | 160A-400.29 |
| §160D-1011. Recordation. | 153A-349.11 | 160A-400.30 |
| §160D-1012. Applicability of procedures to approve debt. | 153A-349.12 | 160A-400.31 |

## ARTICLE 11. Building Code Enforcement

| CHAPTER 160D | CHAPTER 153A | CHAPTER 160A |
|---|---|---|
| §160D-1101. Definitions. | 153A-350<br>153A-350.1 | 160A-442 |
| §160D-1102. Building code administration. | 153A-351 | 1160A-411 |
| §160D-1103. Qualifications of inspectors. | 153A-351.1 | 160A-411.1 |
| §160D-1104. Duties and responsibilities. | 153A-352 | 160A-412 |
| §160D-1105. Other arrangements for inspections. | 153A-353 | 160A-413 |
| §160D-1106. Alternative inspection method for component or element. | -- | 160A-413.5 |
| §160D-1107. Mutual aid contracts. | -- | 160A-413.6 |
| §160D-1108. Conflicts of interest. | 153A-355 | 160A-415 |
| §160D-1109. Failure to perform duties. | 153A-356 | 160A-416 |
| §160D-1110. Building permits. | 153A-357 | 160A-417 |
| §160D-1111. Expiration of building permits. | 153A-358 | 160A-418 |
| §160D-1112. Changes in work. | 153A-359 | 160A-419 |
| §160D-1113. Inspections of work in progress. | 153A-360 | 160A-420 |
| §160D-1114. Appeals of stop orders. | 153A-361 | 160A-421 |
| §160D-1115. Revocation of building permits. | 153A-362 | 160A-422 |
| §160D-1116. Certificates of compliance; temporary certificates of occupancy. | 153A-363 | 160A-423 |
| §160D-1117. Periodic inspections. | 153A-364 | 160A-424 |
| §160D-1118. Defects in buildings to be corrected. | 153A-365 | 160A-425 |
| §160D-1119. Unsafe buildings condemned. | 153A-366 | 160A-426 |
| §160D-1120. Removing notice from condemned buildings. | 153A-367 | 160A-427 |
| §160D-1121. Action in event of failure to take corrective action. | 153A-368 | 160A-428 |
| §160D-1122. Order to take corrective action. | 153A-369 | 160A-429 |
| §160D-1123. Appeal; finality of order if not appealed. | 153A-370 | 160A-430 |
| §160D-1124. Failure to comply with order. | 153A-371 | 160A-431 |
| §160D-1125. Enforcement. | 153A-372 | 160A-432 |
| §160D-1126. Records and reports. | 153A-373 | 160A-433 |
| §160D-1127. Appeals. | 153A-374 | 160A-434 |

| CHAPTER 160D | CHAPTER 153A | CHAPTER 160A |
|---|---|---|
| §160D-1128. Firelimits. | 153A-375 | 160A-435 |
|  |  | 160A-436 |
|  |  | 160A-437 |
|  |  | 160A-438 |
| §160D-1129. Regulation authorized as to repair, closing, and demolition of nonresidential buildings or structures;order of public officer. | -- | 160A-439 |
| §160D-1130. Vacant building receivership. | -- | 160A-439.1 |

## ARTICLE 12. Minimum Housing Codes

| | | |
|---|---|---|
| §160D-1201. Authorization. | -- | 160A-441 |
| §160D-1202. Definitions. | -- | 160A-442 |
| §160D-1203. Ordinance authorized as to repair, closing, and demolition; order of public officer. | -- | 160A-443 |
| §160D-1204. Heat source required. | -- | 160A-443.1 |
| §160D-1205. Standards. | -- | 160A-444 |
| §160D-1206. Service of complaints and orders. | -- | 160A-445 |
| §160D-1207. Periodic inspections. | 153A-364 | 160A-424 |
| §160D-1208. Remedies. | -- | 160A-446 |
| §160D-1209. Compensation to owners of condemned properties. | -- | 160A-447 |
| §160D-1210. Additional powers of public officer. | -- | 160A-448 |
| §160D-1211. Administration of ordinance. | -- | 160A-449 |
| §160D-1212. Supplemental nature of Article. | -- | 160A-450 |

## ARTICLE 13. Additional Authority

### Part 1. Open Space Acquisition

| | | |
|---|---|---|
| §160D-1301. Legislative intent. | -- | 160A-401 |
| §160D-1302. Finding of necessity. | -- | 160A-402 |
| § 160D-1303. Local governments authorized to acquire and reconvey real property. | -- | 160A-403 |
| §160D-1304. Joint action by governing body. | -- | 160A-404 |
| §160D-1305. Powers of governing body. | -- | 160A-405 |
| §160D-1306. Appropriations authorized. | -- | 160A-406 |
| §160D-1307. Definitions. |  | 160A-407 |

### Part 2. Community Development

| | | |
|---|---|---|
| §160D-1311. Community development programs and activities. | 153A-376 | 160A-456 |
| §160D-1312. Acquisition and disposition of property for redevelopment. | 153A-377 | 160A-457 |

# Appendix 5
# Location of Prior Statutes in Chapter 160D

Updated to August 17, 2020

| CHAPTER 160A | CHAPTER 153A | CHAPTER 160D |
|---|---|---|
| **ARTICLE 1. Definitions and Statutory Construction (most also retained in 160A/153A)** | **ARTICLE 1** | |
| §160A-1. Application and meaning of terms. | 153A-1 | 160D-102 |
| §160A-2. Effect upon prior laws. | 153A-2 | 160D-111 |
| §160A-3. General laws supplementary to charters. | 153A-3 | 160D-102; 111 |
| §160A-4. Broad construction. | 153A-4 | 160D-110 |
| §160A-4.1. Notice of new fees and fee increases; public comment period. | -- | 160D-800 |
| §160A-5. Statutory references deemed amended to conform to Chapter 160D. | 153A-5 | 160D-111 |
| **ARTICLE 19. Planning and Regulation of Development** | **ARTICLE 18** | |
| *Part 1. General Provisions* | | |
| §160A-360. Territorial jurisdiction. | 153A-320 | 160D-200; 202; 903 |
| §160A-360.1. Permit choice. | | 160D-108(b) |
| §160A-361. Planning boards. | 153A-321 | 160D-301 |
| §160A-362. Extraterritorial representation. | -- | 160D-307 |
| §160A-363. Supplemental powers. | 153A-322 | 160D-102; 103; 106; 502; |
| §160A-364. Procedure for adopting, amending, or repealing ordinances under Article. | 153A-323 | 160D-601 |
| §160A-364.1. Statute of limitations. | 153A-348 | 160D-1405 |

| CHAPTER 160A | CHAPTER 153A | CHAPTER 160D |
|---|---|---|
| §160A-388. Board of adjustment. | 153A-345.1 | 160D-1-9(d); 302; 403(b); 405; 406; 702; 705; 1405 |
| §160A-389. Remedies. | -- | 160D-404(c) |
| §160A-390. Conflict with other laws. | 153A-346 | 160D-706 |
| §160A-391. Other statutes not repealed. | -- | -- |
| §160A-392. Part applicable to buildings constructed by State and its subdivisions; exception. | 153A-347 | 160D-913 |
| §160A-393. Appeals in the nature of certiorari. | 153A-349 | 160D-1-2; 1402 |
| §160A-393.1. Civil action for declaratory relief, injunctive relief, other remedies; joinder of complaint and petition for writ of certiorari in certain cases | | 160D-1403.1 |
| §160A-393.2. No estoppel effect when challenging development conditions. | | 160D-1403.2 |
| §160A-394. Reserved. | -- | -- |
| §§160A-395 through 160A-399: Repealed. | -- | -- |
| §§160A-399.1 through 160A-400: Repealed. | -- | -- |
| ***Part 3C. Historic Districts and Landmarks*** | -- | ***ARTICLE 9, PART 4*** |
| §160A-400.1. Legislative findings. | -- | 160D-940 |
| §160A-400.2. Exercise of powers by counties as well as cities. | -- | -- |
| §160A-400.3. Character of historic district defined. | -- | 160D-944 |
| §160A-400.4. Designation of historic districts. | -- | 160D-944 |
| §160A-400.5. Designation of landmarks; adoption of an ordinance; criteria for designation. | -- | 160D-945 |
| §160A-400.6. Required landmark designation procedure. | -- | 160D-946 |
| §160A-400.7. Historic Preservation Commission. | -- | 160D-303; 941 |
| §160A-400.8. Powers of the Historic Preservation Commission. | -- | 160D-942 |
| §160A-400.9. Certificate of appropriateness required. | -- | 160D-102; 947 |
| §160A-400.10. Conflict with other laws. | -- | 160D-951 |
| §160A-400.11. Remedies. | -- | 160D-404(c) |
| §160A-400.12. Appropriations. | -- | 160D-943 |
| §160A-400.13. Certain changes not prohibited. | -- | 160D-948 |
| §160A-400.14. Delay in demolition of landmarks and buildings within historic district. | -- | 160D-949 |

| CHAPTER 160A | CHAPTER 153A | CHAPTER 160D |
|---|---|---|
| §160A-400.51A. Local authority. | 153A-349.52 | 160D-932 |
| §160A-400.52. Construction of new wireless support structures or substantial modifications of wireless support structures. | 153A-349.53 | 160D-933 |
| §160A-400.53. Collocation and eligible facilities requests of wireless support structures. | 153A-349.54 | 160D-934 |
| §160A-400.54 through 160A-400.58. Reserved. | | |
| *Part 4. Acquisition of Open Space* | | *ARTICLE 13, PART 1* |
| §160A-401. Legislative intent. | -- | 160D-1301 |
| §160A-402. Finding of necessity. | -- | 160D-1302 |
| §160A-403. Counties or cities authorized to acquire and reconvey real property. | -- | 160D-1303 |
| §160A-404. Joint action by governing bodies. | -- | 160D-1304 |
| §160A-405. Powers of governing bodies. | -- | 160D-1305 |
| §160A-406. Appropriations authorized. | -- | 160D-1306 |
| §160A-407. Definitions. | -- | 160D-1307 |
| §§160A-408 through 160A-410. Reserved. | -- | -- |
| *Part 5. Building Inspection* | | *ARTICLE 11* |
| "Building" defined. | 153A-350 | 160D-1101 |
| Tribal lands. | 153A-350.1 | 160D-1101 |
| §160A-411. Inspection department. | 153A-351 | 160D-402(b); 404(c); 1102 |
| §160A-411.1. Qualifications of inspectors. | 153A-351.1 | 160D-1103 |
| §160A-412. Duties and responsibilities. | 153A-352 | 160D-402(b); 1104 |
| §160A-413. Joint inspection department; other arrangements. | 153A-353 | 160D-402(c); 1105 |
| §160A-413.5. Alternate inspection method for component or element | -- | 160D-1106 |
| §160A-413.6. Mutual aid contracts. | 153A-353.1 | 160D-1107 |
| §160A-414. Financial support; fee collection, accounting, and use limitation. | 153A-354 | 160D-402(d) |
| §160A-415. Conflicts of interest. | 153A-355 | 160D-109(c); 1108 |
| §160A-416. Failure to perform duties. | 153A-356 | 160D-1109 |
| §160A-417. Permits. | 153A-357 | 160D-403; 1110 |
| §160A-418. Time limitations on validity of permits. | 153A-358 | 160D-403(c); 1111 |
| §160A-419. Changes in work. | 153A-359 | 160D-403(d); 1112 |
| §160A-420. Inspections of work in progress. | 153A-360 | 160D-403(e); 1113 |

| CHAPTER 160A | CHAPTER 153A | CHAPTER 160D |
|---|---|---|
| §160A-421. Stop orders. | 153A-361 | 160D-404(b); 1114 |
| §160A-422. Revocation of permits. | 153A-362 | 160D-403(f); 1115 |
| §160A-423. Certificates of compliance. | 153A-363 | 160D-403(g); 1116 |
| §160A-424. Periodic inspections. | 153A-364 | 160D-1117, 1207 |
| §160A-425. Defects in buildings to be corrected. | 153A-365 | 160D-1118 |
| §160A-425.1: Repealed. | -- | -- |
| §160A-426. Unsafe buildings condemned in localities. | 153A-366 | 160D-1119 |
| §160A-427. Removing notice from condemned building. | 153A-367 | 160D-1120 |
| §160A-428. Action in event of failure to take corrective action. | 153A-368 | 160D-1121 |
| §160A-429. Order to take corrective action. | 153A-369 | 160D-1122 |
| §160A-430. Appeal; finality of order if not appealed. | 153A-370 | 160D-1123 |
| §160A-431. Failure to comply with order. | 153A-371 | 160D-1124 |
| §160A-432. Enforcement. | 153A-372 | 160D-1125 |
| §160A-433. Records and reports. | 153A-373 | 160D-1126 |
| §160A-434. Appeals in general. | 153A-374 | 160D-1127 |
| §160A-435. Establishment of fire limits. | 153A-375 | 160D-1128 |
| §160A-436. Restrictions within primary fire limits. | -- | 160D-1128 |
| §160A-437. Restriction within secondary fire limits. | -- | 160D-1128 |
| §160A-438. Failure to establish primary fire limits. | -- | 160D-1128 |
| §160A-439. Ordinance authorized as to repair, closing, and demolition of nonresidential buildings or structures; order of public officer. | 153A-372.1 | 160D-1129 |
| §160A-439.1. Vacant building receivership | | 160D-1130 |
| §160A-440. Reserved. | -- | -- |
| *Part 6. Minimum Housing Standards* | | *ARTICLE 12* |
| §160A-441. Exercise of police power authorized. | -- | 160D-1201 |
| §160A-442. Definitions. | -- | 160D-102; 1101; 1202 |
| §160A-443. Ordinance authorized as to repair, closing, and demolition; order of public officer. | -- | 160D-1203 |
| §160A-443.1. Heat source required. | -- | 160D-1204 |
| §160A-444. Standards. | -- | 160D-1205 |
| §160A-445. Service of complaints and orders. | -- | 160D-1206 |
| §160A-446. Remedies. | -- | 160D-305; 1208 |
| §160A-447. Compensation to owners of condemned property. | -- | 160D-1209 |
| §160A-448. Additional powers of public officer. | -- | 160D-1210 |

| CHAPTER 160A | CHAPTER 153A | CHAPTER 160D |
|---|---|---|
| §160A-449. Administration of ordinance. | -- | 160D-1211 |
| §160A-450. Supplemental nature of Part. | -- | 160D-1212 |
| **Part 7. Community Appearance Commissions** | | **ARTICLE 9, PART 5** |
| §160A-451. Membership and appointment of commission; joint commission. | -- | 160D-304 |
| §160A-452. Powers and duties of commission. | -- | 160D-960 |
| §160A-453. Staff services; advisory council. | -- | 160D-961 |
| §160A-454. Annual report. | -- | 160D-962 |
| §160A-455. Receipt and expenditure of funds. | -- | 160D-963 |
| **Part 8. Miscellaneous Powers** | | |
| §160A-456. Community development programs and activities. | 153A-376 | 160D-1311 |
| §160A-457. Acquisition and disposition of property for redevelopment. | 153A-377 | 160D-1312 |
| §160A-457.1. Urban Development Action Grants. | -- | 160D-1313 |
| §160A-457.2. Urban homesteading programs. | -- | 160D-1314 |
| §160A-458. Erosion and sedimentation control. | -- | 160D-922 |
| §160A-458.1. Floodway regulations. | -- | 160D-923 |
| §160A-458.2. Mountain ridge protection. | 153A-448 | 160D-924 |
| §160A-458.3. Downtown development projects. | -- | 160D-1315 |
| §160A-458.4. Designation of transportation corridor official maps. | -- | 160D-916 |
| §160A-458.5. Restriction of certain forestry activities prohibited. | 153A-452 | 160D-921 |
| §160A-459. Stormwater control. | 153A-454 | 160D-925 |
| §160A-459.1. Program to finance energy improvements. | 153A-455 | 160D-1320 |
| Low- and moderate-income housing programs | 153A-378 | 160D-1316 |

## Others

| | | |
|---|---|---|
| §160A-181.1. Adult businesses. | -- | 160D-902 |
| §160A-199. Outdoor advertising. | 153A-143 | 160D-912 |
| §160A-201. Solar collectors. | 153A-143 | 160D-914 |
| §168-20 to -22. Family care homes. | -- | 160D-907 |

# Index

demolition
    candidates for, 6, 7t
    order to remove or demolish, 35–36
Dillon's rule, 12–13, 24n8, 54n128
direct effectuation. *See* effectuation by local government
due process issues, 16, 24n15, 24n21, 39, 46–47n15, 48n44, 52n93
effectuation by local government
    procedures for, 57–58
    of removal or demolition, using minimum housing ordinance, 36
    of repair or improvement
        after vacation and closure, 37, 51n74
        using general police power, 18–19
        using minimum housing ordinance, 37
ends-means reasonableness test for exercise of general police power. *See under* general police power
enforcement
    by direct effectuation. *See* effectuation by local government
    of general police power, 18–19
    joint application of general police power and minimum housing standards, 57–58
    of minimum housing standards
        abandonment of intent to repair procedure, 38–39, 66t
        of orders to remove or demolish, 36
        of orders to repair, 37–38
        repair orders more than one year old, 39
extraterritorial jurisdiction. 46n7

fees, administrative, 19–20, 41–42, 59
fines and civil penalties
    differentiation of, 20
    enforcement of local ordinances enacted under general police power by, 18
    joint application of general police power and minimum housing standards, 58–59
    minimum housing ordinances unable to impose, 42
    recoupment of costs of regulatory activities via, 20
    for unlawful occupation of vacated and closed dwelling, 54n124
"fit for human habitation," order to repair in order to render dwelling, 36. *See also* "unfit for human habitation"

foreclosed properties, vacant or abandoned. *See* vacant or abandoned dwellings; vacate and close order

Fourth Amendment, U.S. Constitution, 33

funding. *See* recoupment of costs of regulatory activities

general police power, 11–30. *See also* joint application of general police power and minimum housing standards
  authority of local government to exercise, 11–15
  case law on application to repair-oriented regulations, 15–18
  ends-means reasonableness test, 13–16
  enforcement of local ordinances enacted under, 18–19
  limitations on, 20–23, 22*t*
  order of abatement, 18
  ordinance-making authority pursuant to, 8n2
  recoupment of costs of regulatory activities, 19–20
  stages of housing conditions, statutory tools for dealing with, 7*t*
  statutory texts, 71–75

"good repair" regulations applicable to nonstructural outward appearance of dwelling, 15–18

green dwelling condition, 5, 7*t*, 20–21, 22, 23*t*, 31

hearings under minimum housing standards, 34–35, 50n55

"home rule" state, North Carolina not regarded as, 24n6

housing codes for repair and maintenance. *See* repair and maintenance regulations

identification of persons to be served with complaints, 33

imposition of conditions or uses on real property, 18

imprisonment under general police power, 18

inspection program, statutory authority for, 8n1

intent to repair, abandonment of. *See* abandonment of intent to repair procedure

investigations, preliminary, 33, 47n18, 68–69*f*

joint application of general police power and minimum housing standards, 55–60
  enforcement and effectuation, 57–58
  enumeration of standards of maintenance, 56–57
  fines and civil penalties, 58–59

strict compliance with notice and hearing requirements, 35
time limits for making repairs, 38, 39, 52–53n95
"unfit for human habitation," defining, 32

new construction requirements, 26n33
nonresidential buildings, repair and maintenance of, 3n4
nonstructural outward appearance of dwelling, "good repair" regulations
    applicable to, 15–18
notice
    affordable housing organizations, notice to
        of remove or demolish order, 36
        of vacate and close order, 37
    of building's unfitness for human habitation, 37
    service of complaint, 33–35
    strict compliance required, 35

orders. *See under* minimum housing standards; general police power,
    order of abatement
outward appearance of dwelling, nonstructural, "good repair" regula-
    tions applicable to, 15–18. *See also* aesthetic considerations
owner-occupied dwellings, "good repair" regulations applied to, 17
owners, identification and service of, 33–34

parties in interest, identification and service of, 33–34
penalties. *See* fines and civil penalties
police power. *See* general police power
preliminary investigations, 33, 47n18, 68–69f
property values
    "broken windows" theory and, 6
    effects of "eyesore" properties on, 1
    "good repair" regulations and, 16, 26–27n37
publication, service of complaints by, 34

reasonable cost percentage, 42–43, 64t
reasonableness
    ends-means reasonableness test for exercise of general police
        power, 13–16
    service of complaints, 33, 47–48n26, 48n32

recoupment of costs of regulatory activities
    joint application of general police power and minimum housing
        standards, 58
    under general police power, 19–20
    under minimum housing standards, 36, 41–42
red dwelling condition, 6, 7t, 21, 22–23, 23t, 31
redevelopment strategies for black and blue properties, 9n7
refusal of service, 34, 48n33
remove or demolish orders, 35–36
rental inspection program, 8n1
repair and maintenance regulations, 1–3
    dwelling defined for purposes of, 3n1
    general police power, 11–30. *See also* general police power
    joint application of general police power and minimum housing
        standards, 55–60. *See also* joint application of general police power
        and minimum housing standards
    minimum housing standards, 31–54. *See also* minimum housing
        standards
    nonresidential buildings, repair and maintenance of, 3n4
    stages of housing conditions, statutory tools for dealing with, 5–9, 7t
repair of dwelling after vacate and closure order, 37, 51n74. *See also* aban-
    donment of intent to repair
repair orders more than one year old, 39
repair orders under minimum housing standards, 36–37, 39

sale of materials and appurtenances, 36
school systems, general police power civil penalties and fines paid over
    to, 20
search and seizure restrictions, Fourth Amendment, U.S.
    Constitution, 33
separate balancing test for exercise of general police power, 14–15, 16, 17,
    25n24
service of complaints under minimum housing standards, 33–34
statutory tools for housing code enforcement. *See* repair and mainte-
    nance regulations
strict compliance with minimum housing ordinance notice and hearing
    requirements, 35
structural soundness and safety, repair-oriented regulations applicable
    to, 15

takings challenges, 16, 26n37

tenant-occupied dwellings, "good repair" regulations applied to, 17

time limits for making repairs, 38, 39, 52–53n95

"unfit for human habitation"
    additional standards for, 43–45
    defined, 32
    determination procedures, 62–63t
    general police powers and, 21, 22, 23
    as legal concept, 5–6, 8n3
    minimum housing standards and, 32
uses or conditions on real property, imposition of, 18

vacant or abandoned dwellings
    "good repair" regulations applied to, 17
    negative externalities resulting from, 1, 25n29
vacate and close order, 35–38
    fines and civil penalties for unlawful occupation of dwelling
        after, 54n124
    repair of dwelling after, 37, 51n74

warrants for preliminary investigations, 33, 47n18, 68–69f

yellow dwelling condition, 5–6, 7t, 20–21, 22, 23t, 31

ISBN-13: 978-1560116622

90000

9 781560 116622

www.ingramcontent.com/pod-product-compliance
Lightning Source LLC
Chambersburg PA
CBHW061829220326
41599CB00027B/5233